The Young Person's Guide to Becoming a Writer

Janet E. Grant

EDITED BY PAMELA ESPELAND

Library of Congress Cataloging-in-Publication Data

Grant, Janet.
    The young person's guide to becoming a writer / Janet E. Grant ; edited by Pamela Espeland.
       p. cm.
    Originally published : White Hall, Va. : Shoe Tree Press, 1991. Includes bibliographical references and index.
    Summary: Provides information on identifying the writer within, creating three-dimensional characters, submitting a manuscript for publication, and other authorship issues.
    ISBN 0-915793-90-3 (pbk. : alk. paper)
    1. Children as authors. 2. Authorship – Handbooks, manuals, etc. – Juvenile literature. [1. Children as authors. 2. Authorship – Handbooks, manuals, etc.]
    I. Espeland, Pamela, 1951–   . II. Title.
PN171.C5G68   1995
808'.02'083–dc20

95-19541
CIP
AC

10 9 8 7 6 5 4 3 2 1

Printed in the United States of America

Cover and book design by MacLean & Tuminelly

Index compiled by Eileen Quam and Theresa Wolner

The storyboard shown on pages 66–67 is © Mark Thurman from *Draw & Write Your Own Picture Book*. Reprinted with permission. Pembroke Publishers, 538 Hood Rd., Markham, Ontario, Canada L3R 3K9. Available in the U.S. from The Wright Group, 19201 120th Avenue NE, Bothell, WA 98011-9512.

FREE SPIRIT PUBLISHING INC.
400 First Avenue North, Suite 616
Minneapolis, MN 55401-1730
(612) 338-2068

Dedication

In memory of Gerald Durrell, the world-famous naturalist
and the first author to make me cry with laughter,
and to the Jersey Wildlife Preservation Trust in the Channel Islands.

Acknowledgments

I am deeply grateful to the following people, who have contributed
to this book in their own unique ways:

Mark Thurman, for his non-stop support, humor, and tennis
prowess;

Sandi Harwood, for coaching me in public relations;

Kathy Henderson, for updating the contest listings;

Lucy LaGrassa and Janyse Lastman, for all our youth creativity
think-tank sessions;

Phillip Coffey and the Jersey Zoo, for believing a zoo committed
to breeding endangered species really needed a writer-in-residence
program;

Judy Galbraith, for caring about good books and young writers;

Pamela Espeland, for making me laugh 3,000 miles away;

All the staff at the International Young Authors' Camp (formerly
the Canadian Young Authors' Camp) and the young writers and
their parents whose demand for exceptional challenges and support
inspired this book;

My own parents and brothers and sisters (Ian, Alan, Jennifer,
and Judith); and

My friends, my ex-cat, Winnie, and Richard, for all their love
and support.

Contents

Foreword

by Linda Valenta, 16
*Linda Valenta attended the International Young Authors' Camp,
founded by Janet E. Grant.*

SHAKESPEARE SAID IT BEST in *Hamlet:* "Words. Words. Words."
Right from the beginning, words shape lives.

It takes a person who loves the art of writing to complicate that
simple concept.

Do you want to be a writer?

Please don't say, "I'm not good enough, my parents say I'm not
supposed to, I couldn't take it, I shouldn't."

Just answer the question: *Do you want to be a writer?*

Thank you.

Whether you said "yes," "no," "maybe," or even if you're one of
those people who doesn't believe in participating with what the writer
is saying...thank you.

Just by reading what I've written, you have made me part of your
life in some way. My voice has entered your mind. You have made me
a writer. A writer without a reader is like an actor without an audience.
No matter how brilliant you may be, if no one is there to listen, you
may as well have never spoken.

The main concern is how to make people listen. How are people
going to sit up and take notice of *you*? That is what this book tries to
explain. Life does not come with full instructions, but sometimes we
need a little guidance. That is what this book hopes to achieve.

We are not creatures of instinct. You don't wake up one morning understanding the molecular theory of matter, just as you don't suddenly notice one day the path to getting published. Both take dedication.

But we're young. We shouldn't worry ourselves with that sort of stuff, right? Then why, at school, does it seem more probable to find someone willing to explain the molecular theory of matter to you than it does to find someone to teach you about the publishing industry, which is as complicated, if not more so, than splitting atoms?

That is what this book and its author, Janet E. Grant, realize. There are no promises, no guarantees; it's still your hard work and love of writing that's going to get you where you want to go. This book is your little kick in the behind, just to get you started. So, without further ado, take it away, Janet!

Introduction

Warning! This is not a creative writing book!

Instead, it encourages you to uncover your own true ability to write, and it gives you some of the tools you'll need along the way. It challenges you to explore new types of writing, work harder at your writing, have fun, and (if you want) produce exceptional pieces, win awards, get published, and make new friends.

The only person who knows what is best for you in your development as a writer is *you*. That's why this book never tells you *how to write*. Instead, it assumes that you want to write, that you're prepared to put some effort into it, and that you may turn your writing into a career someday.

In fact, this book is a kind of career guide. It is based on research with two groups of people:

- professional authors, and

- highly motivated young writers (who tested each and every exercise and gave me constant feedback on what really worked).

It includes information on finding your writing style, finding other writers, trying various types of writing, getting feedback and support from friends as well as adults (parents, teachers, librarians, etc.), preparing your manuscript for submission to a publisher, finding the right publishers, getting paid, and more topics of interest to serious young writers.

Each topic could be an entire book by itself. I have tried to introduce them in the simplest way I can so you can start learning and doing the exercises immediately. The exercises, titled "Writer's Notebook," will provide you with vital information. Don't skip them! With this book – and your own talent, initiative, curiosity, and skill – you can become a writer. (Naturally, you will need something to use for your Writer's Notebook. This can be anything you choose – a blank book, a spiral-bound notebook, a three-ring binder, a scrapbook – as long as it works for you and you use it to do the exercises.)

I have worked with young writers for many years – as director of the International Young Authors' Camp, in schools and universities in North America and Great Britain, in various writer-in-residence programs, and as a writing coach – and I am convinced that each young writer has something unique to contribute, whether it is in book form, article form, book review form, or whatever. Teenagers, in general, have a voice that needs to be heard by adults, other teenagers, and children.

I have never held that young people are our future. Somehow that conjures up an untrue picture of generations of adults who have made huge mistakes and are too stupid or irresponsible to correct them. I hold that teenagers are our (my) partners. We work together. When I don't know about "what is really true" for you, I wait for you to tell me, and vice versa. (I think it's called *respect*.) Also, I have a great memory of my childhood and teenage years, but I can't speak *authentically* about what it is like to be a teenager right now. In fact, that's why this book is laced with contributions from teenagers. It was a partnership to produce the best book possible in an area where I felt that good, useful information was missing.

Two brief notes before we begin:

- Because I have studied, taught, written, and coached young writers in many places, I have found many wonderful resources for writers: market guides, books by writers, and other sources of information and inspiration. Some are published in the United States, others in England, Canada, or Australia. I have listed many of them in this book. If there is a title that interests you but it is not published in your country, you might check with a librarian or your local bookstore to see if it is available anyway. Sometimes books published in one country are also published in others, in slightly different editions; sometimes books published in one country are picked up by distributors in other countries. If you can't find a particular title anywhere, look for other titles on the same subject or related subjects. As you start searching for books about writing, you'll be amazed at how many you discover – in bookstores and in libraries. (One more word of advice about books: I have listed the most current editions available at the time this book was published. You may find newer editions. Always use the latest edition you can find.)

- The study of the development of talent in young writers is a relatively new field. The path is being blazed with the help of professional writers and many, many young writers not much older than you. If you would like to contribute your own experiences, insights, or comments to this ongoing "practical study," please write to me in care of my publisher: Free Spirit Publishing Inc., 400 First Avenue North, Suite 616, Minneapolis, MN 55401-1730, U.S.A. I hope to hear from you.

Janet E. Grant
London, England

CHAPTER ONE

The Land of the Imagination

You HAVE JUST BEEN to a local sports event or a friend's party. You saw or heard something that wasn't very unusual but was emotional. You mull it over in your mind and replay the events. You begin to exaggerate the characters and their dialogue, and you imagine what would happen if you changed the human characters to fictional beings from another planet. You start to consider all the possible outcomes. A kernel of a story is born.

You are walking home in the evening. The full moon is out. You remember that the moon is not just a moon. In the land of the imagination, it is the place a cow jumped over. It is a place where the man in the moon lives. You look up again at the moon, and one image or many images come into your mind. You play with the one that fits best. You put words to it. You repeat those words to yourself, then let them slip away. Or you carefully take them home with you and record them in your journal.

You are sitting by a river, daydreaming. The river sounds a particular way. Before you know it, you are transported into another world where the sound of the river is not just a sound, it is anything you dare to make it. You can transform it. You can re-create it. Each time, you do it a little differently.

Just as the young artist learns to draw by seeing the space around an object, rather than just the object, the young writer learns to write by observing and searching for the not-so-obvious truth, then mixing it with the imagination. For when writers play with their imaginations, they are playing with the questions "What is true?" and "What is false?"

People, places, perceptions, and thoughts can be played with, captured, transformed, and re-created – such are the extraordinary laws of the imagination. When people are really aware of the power of the creative imagination, they feel as if they can walk through walls. Johnathon, 14, describes it as "an escape from the present world, into a world that's all my own. Mine to create as I want it. A world where I call the shots and make the rules." Sigrid, 13, says, "I love writing because it gives me a chance for my imagination to go wild."

The young person who loves to make up stories or record events in an interesting way moves naturally in and out of the land of the imagination. You already like to imagine things and, when possible, write them down. My wish is to encourage you to write down what you see in your own unique way, the way that best serves your talents and interests – whether you consider yourself a writer or not.

"Most of the basic material a writer works with is acquired before the age of fifteen."

Willa Cather, author of O PIONEERS!

How Do You Know If You Are a Writer?

There are signs. Perhaps when you do the inkblot test (a test in which you are given an inkblot and asked to come up with as many things as you see it could be), you cover two sides of the page. Or you daydream easily. Bob Munsch, a Canadian author and storyteller *extraordinaire*, says he daydreamed all the time, especially in the classroom.

Or perhaps you keep a diary to record events, people, and feelings. Lucy Maud Montgomery, creator of *Anne of Green Gables,* wrote in her diary every day from the age of nine. She felt that not to write daily in her diary would be as bad as not washing her face!

Or perhaps you have a passion for a particular hobby or subject – such as hockey, history, or current events – and you keep thinking of ways to write an article or story based on your knowledge or experience.

Taking the Same Steps

All over the world, young writers take similar steps in pursuing an interest in writing about things that matter to them. As one young writer in Copenhagen, Denmark, finds a weakness in her main character that she can exploit in her plot, another young writer in Amsterdam, Holland, awakes with the solution to a plot that had been difficult to solve the night before. As one young writer walks to a writers' club at his local library in Montreal, Canada, plucking up his courage to join a club with kids five years older than he is, another young writer in western Australia takes a biography of a famous writer off a library shelf in order to find out what steps she can take. Meanwhile, a young writer in Washington, D.C., jumps for joy because her first article has been accepted for publication, and another writer in the Lake District of England looks proudly at his poem in a local magazine!

Special Concerns

Young writers who wish to develop their writing talent have their own special set of concerns and needs. As avid readers, they are eager to find more challenging books. Comfortable with expressing themselves on paper, they are willing to do practical exercises to bring new depths to their writing. Ready to make new friends who also share an interest in writing, they are open to seeking out unusual opportunities to meet other young writers who may be younger or older than they are. Faced inevitably with making a first career decision, they need a simple explanation of how a writer makes enough money to earn a living, along with other information about the day-to-day realities of being a writer.

Four Ways to Develop Your Writing Talent

In his book, *Developing Talent in Young People,* Benjamin S. Bloom writes: "All the talented individuals we interviewed invested considerable practice and training time, which rivaled the time devoted to school or any other activity. And this time in many ways was more intense and rewarding than the time they put into almost anything else." (For more about Benjamin Bloom's book, see pages 161–162.)

"In the past I tried discussing the art of capturing good dialogue and outrageous characters at parties, only to be shunned to the vegetable and dip table. I was a closet writer."

Christine Klich, 18

All young writers know instinctively that reading books is one way to develop their abilities as writers. But besides reading, and writing occasionally, it is not particularly clear what else they should do.

Yet if you play a competitive sport after school, you already are familiar with doing drills and practicing your skills. If you have attended art classes, you know that you can look around for special classes and instructors. In fact, you can use your experience in just about any other field (such as sports or the arts) to help you become a writer.

Look at your friends who have interests in piano, hockey, tennis, or skiing. They have drills or practices to do. They work with coaches. They sometimes even give recitals or perform in competitions.

Can some of these ideas be adapted to writing? Of course they can. Perhaps the steps to becoming a writer are not that mysterious after all.

Ask yourself these questions:

- "Has anyone encouraged me to find out what writing I have a natural tendency for?"
- "Has anyone shown me ways to develop and control characters and plots?"
- "Has anyone encouraged me to write regularly each day?"
- "Has anyone encouraged me to find a mentor?"
- "Has anyone advised me to join a writing club or writing organization?"

If you answer "no" to all of these questions, don't be discouraged. The fact is, most young writers will respond to these questions with an emphatic "no." If you can answer "yes" to one or more of these questions, then someone else has already taken an interest in developing your writing talent. The next steps are up to you.

Over my years of working with young writers (both in schools and privately), I have found that there are four things young writers can do that will help improve their writing significantly.

1. Learn about different types of writing.

A *genre* (pronounced "zhän-rə") is a category of literary work with distinctive characteristics. Each genre – whether fantasy, mystery, adventure, horror, science fiction, humor, biography, romance, or how-to books – has a particular set of "rules" for what can work and what doesn't seem to work. Each genre also has a particular history. For example, some people figure that Charlotte Brontë, who wrote *Jane Eyre* in 1847, launched the genre of the romantic suspense story.

Learn how the genres have developed over the years. This can help if you ever get stuck wondering, "Why can't I seem to write anything longer than a short story?" "Why do my plays sound like documentaries?" "Why did I place tenth in the competition rather than first?"

2. Surround yourself with good support for your writing.

Get feedback on your work. Have someone to talk with or write to about writing. Figure out the best support network for you. Find out about young writers' clubs, mentors, pen pals, and special writing classes and camps with professional authors.

3. Set aside a regular writing time that fits in with your schedule.

What should you do with this time? Learn to expand your observation powers and imagination. Play with settings, characters, words, and storyboards. (To learn about storyboards, see Chapter Four.) The way you perceive the world is unique. But are you getting it down on paper?

4. Learn about the opportunities in the publishing industry specifically for young writers.

Entering and winning certain competitions for young writers can help you get your first book published. Sending off articles to publications that specialize in publishing work by young writers can teach you important skills, especially discipline. And with the right information, you can improve your chances of being published and avoid the most common mistakes new writers make when starting out on their careers.

• • •

As a writer, you can give yourself practice time. You can read books about writing, which will help you to develop better characters and control your plots. You can go to writing classes, find your own writing coach or mentor, read from your work at special reading nights, and enter writing competitions. You can develop your writing talent.

Think for a moment of what you have done up until now to develop your writing ability. Have you written as much as you have wanted to write? Have you really given yourself a chance to explore the different types of writing? Have you found some friends who also write?

Rate Yourself

Take your Writer's Notebook and write on the top of the first page, "Four Ways to Develop My Writing Talent." Then copy these four ways in your notebook:

___ 1. Learn about different types of writing.

___ 2. Surround myself with good support for my writing.

___ 3. Set aside a regular writing time.

___ 4. Learn about opportunities in the publishing industry.

Now rate yourself. For each of the four ways, give yourself a 3 for "Excellent," a 2 for "Fair," and a 1 for "Needs Work." If a really good idea comes to you about how you could improve in any of these areas, jot it down in your Writer's Notebook. (Throughout this book, you'll find activities and suggestions on how to improve in all four ways of developing your writing talent.)

An Afternoon with Your Favorite Authors

It would be nice to meet all of our favorite authors in person, but sometimes it just isn't possible. They may live far away. They may have lived 100 years ago! But that doesn't mean you can't read about your favorite authors.

Think of three writers you would like to know more about. Go to your local library or the media center at your school and ask the librarian to help you find biographies, autobiographies, or short biographical sketches of the three authors.

In the United States and Canada, good places to start are with one or more volumes from these two series. Each contains fascinating short references to authors from all countries:

- *Authors and Artists for Young Adults, Vol. 5: A Biographical Guide to Novelists, Poets, Playwrights, Screenwriters, Lyricists, Illustrators, Cartoonists, Animators, and Other Creative Artists,* edited by Agnes Garrett and Helga P. McCue (Detroit: Gale Research Inc., 1990).

- *Yesterday's Authors of Books for Children: Facts and Pictures about Authors and Illustrators of Books for Young People* by Anne Commire (Detroit: Gale Research Inc., 1977).

In Australia, you can read:

- *No Kidding: Top Writers for Young People Talk about Their Work* by Agnes Neuenhausen (Chippendale: Macmillan/PEN, 1991). Interviews with 12 of Australia's top writers of teenage fiction, from Allan Baillie to Patricia Wrightson.

In Canada, you might also look for:

- *Presenting* CANSCAIP, edited by Barbara Greenwood (Markham: Pembroke Publishers, 1990). Profiles Canadian children's artists (authors, illustrators, and performers) from Gordon Korman to Monica Hughes.

- *A Riot of Writers* by Terrance Dicks (Markham: Pembroke Publishers, 1993). Profiles writers of English literature, from Chaucer to Shakespeare, from the Brontës to Ernest Hemingway.

In Great Britain, try to locate:

- *Twentieth-Century Crime and Mystery Writers,* edited by Lesley Henderson (London: St. James Press, 1991).

- *Twentieth-Century Romance and Historical Writers,* 3rd edition, edited by Aruna Vasudenan (London: St. James Press, 1994).

- *Who's Who in Horror and Fantasy Fiction,* compiled by Mike Ashley (London: Elm Tree Books, 1977).

Then find a comfortable armchair and curl up for the afternoon. You may discover some interesting similarities and differences between you and your favorite authors, or you might just learn some fascinating facts about their lives.

"A writer is a foreign country."
Marguerite Duras in PRACTICALITIES

When I was doing research on people involved in successful films and musicals, I found a whole assortment of unusual anecdotes. For example, Jim Henson was just about 18 when he landed his first job on television using puppets. When British actor and director Kenneth Branagh was 17, he spent time every night reading back issues of theater magazines. Stephen Sondheim had Oscar Hammerstein II as a surrogate father, and Oscar critiqued Stephen's first attempts at writing for the theater.

In your Writer's Notebook, you may wish to jot down some of the activities your favorite authors did that you might like to try, or anything else you want to remember about them.

CHAPTER TWO

Identifying the Writer Within

TAKING TIME TO SIT DOWN and think about the world is what makes us all writers. We write in response to the events happening around us, the people talking around us, or the social events shaping the planet. But we also need to take time to look at ourselves. We need to ask, "Why do I write?" "What exactly am I trying to say? To myself? To others?" These are important questions. You may come up with one answer one day and an even clearer answer a few months from now.

What makes you different from the writers in your class? What makes your writing different from that of any other person in your school? If you've had your writing published in your community, what makes you different from, say, the woman down the street from you who writes? What makes you different from Roald Dahl, Judy Blume, Gary Paulsen, J.R.R. Tolkien, Cynthia Voigt, Isaac Asimov, Astrid Lindgren, or any other writer, for that matter?

Each writer has his or her own style of writing. Who you are plays an important role in your writing: the types of writing you like doing best, the problems you set up for your characters to solve, your choice of settings, the imagery in your poetry, your angle in a sports biography, and so on.

Writer's Bluff

How well do you really know your favorite writer? Pretend for a moment that you have been given a page of writing from a book by one of your favorite writers. Neither the title nor the writer's name appears anywhere on the page. The characters' names (if any) have been blotted out.

How could you identify your favorite writer? Does he or she write in a particular way, or write about a special subject? Jot down your thoughts in your Writer's Notebook.

Now try another favorite writer, poet, or playwright. Again, what would be the telltale clue that would identify him or her? Add these to your Writer's Notebook.

After a while, you should be able to tell different writers apart, just as you can tell different rock groups or classical composers apart.

With some imagination and preparation, you can make this exercise into a game to play with friends. Some very successful authors have actually taught themselves to write by literally copying paragraphs, chapters, and whole books by other successful writers. This certainly is one way to learn first-hand another's style, form, rhythm and voice.

The Reason You Write

The reasons young people write are as varied as young people themselves. Because you are an individual, you have your own unique or personalized reasons for doing things.

Young writers like to somehow make sense of what is happening to them in day-to-day life, sometimes through expressing their emotions. They like to use writing as a means of escape from the over-stimulus of the outside world. They like to use writing as a vehicle for communicating important information, either a story or a series of thoughts. Affecting the reader by either entertaining or teaching is an important motive in writing.

Listen to the motives behind two well-known authors who were published in their teens:

- "I stress the significance of life before 21. I don't look at my characters' childhoods as a time for growth and development or as a carefree interlude until one is forced to enter the real world in later life. This is the real world full of powerful friendships, strong values, fears, triumphs and failures." Gordon Korman, author of *This Can't Be Happening at MacDonald Hall*

- "I like to express my feelings, stretch my imagination, and earn money." S.E. Hinton, author of *The Outsiders*

Following are some reasons other young writers write. As you read them, watch for clues to what each young writer is concerned about. There are hints of the characters they want to write about, the problems that intrigue them, the importance of working with their imagination, and the need for expressing emotional concerns.

- "I love to write because it is a way to express myself without limiting myself to something. I can go beyond the limits in writing and use my imagination any way I want." Jodie, 12

- "I write as a means of enjoyment. I enjoy expressing myself on paper and I also enjoy being able to use my talent in cartooning." Andrew, 13

- "To me, writing is a means of self-expression as well as a means of escaping from reality into a world of fantasy, discovery and tranquillity.... To be sensitive towards the environment is the philosophy behind good writing." Zahra, 15

- "I believe that children have new ideas to share but lack the experience to express themselves. In between two worlds are the young adults who should be given a chance to teach the world untarnished values. If they succeed, the world becomes better. If they fail, they will learn and try again." Derek, 18

- "In the world we live in today, there is a lack of imagination. People are very scientific. You have to use imagination to give a different perspective of the world." Dave, 14

- "My work is a reflection of my life and events in it. It keeps me from punching walls. It allows me to release the ideas which get caught in my head, leaving my mind stuck in a perpetual 'rinse' cycle." Jessie, 17

- "I want my readers to feel everything I've put into my writing, and I want them to feel close to my characters. I want to leave an impression. And I don't want to make people laugh or cry; I want them to do both." Liz, 16

- "The ordinary person, the one who is not readily noticed, the person who is not full of Hollywood glitter and glitz…this is the character who brings forth the real revelation of life." Christine, 19

- "I want to make the impossible believable. I want to make people look over their shoulders. If that means scaring them, all the better. I want to educate and entertain by bringing the surreal to people's front door. If nothing else, they must almost believe what I say, and be affected. I must leave my mark." Peter, 15

Let's take the last example, Peter's, to look briefly at what philosophies can tell you. What are some of the clues you think Peter's writing philosophy is signaling? What type of stories do you think he writes? If you guessed thriller/horror, you're right! Peter is also asking for his readers to give him feedback that he has indeed made the impossible believable. He is willing to dig deep into his characters' motives and the way life deals their hand.

Re-read the other young writers' reasons for writing. What type of writing do you think inspires them?

The Reason You Write

Why do you write? Have you ever tried to express why you write by actually writing it down? This doesn't have to be super-serious. It's simply that focusing brings clarity to what you do. You may know what inspires you to write right now, or you may need time to come up with a statement that sums it up for you. It may help to ask yourself these questions:

- "What inspires me about writing?"
- "What do I really care about?"
- "What do I want my readers to be left with when they read my writing?" (A new understanding of how important relatives are? A good mood after laughing at your jokes?)
- "What makes certain books important to me?" (Do they make you learn things? Do they express ideas you care about?)
- "How do I see the role of books in a society's development?" (As pure entertainment? As reflecting what society can't see?)

In your Writer's Notebook, write a sentence or two describing your own reason(s) for writing. You can call this your *writing philosophy*. As time passes, you should look back at your philosophy and consider whether it has changed in any way. Record these changes in your notebook.

MY WRITING PHILOSOPHY IS:

To make the reader ask questions of himself/herself.

It is a challenge in a world which, without these

questions, would quickly stagnate.

REVISION (1 YEAR LATER):

To make young adults question their role in society.

To make use of real events rather than science fiction.

A Peace Break

Have people forgotten what peace of mind is? What gentleness is? Have they lost their ability to look inside themselves? Sometimes it seems that way.

Who you are *inside* is as important as who you are *outside*. And, quite frankly, you already know that, otherwise you wouldn't be developing your own inner voice as a writer.

In each of the reasons for writing given by the young writers on pages 19–20, there is a sense that the young writer has found a quiet place inside – whether a place to reflect or a place to create from doesn't really matter. Connecting with that quiet place inside is essential.

In your Writer's Notebook, write down the following words and what they mean to you.

- wisdom

- peace

- gentleness.

Do you think you have these qualities? How might cultivating these qualities help your writing?

Try to take a "peace break" of at least 15 minutes each day. Turn off your mind and just sit still. You might write your insights from these sessions in your Writer's Notebook.

• • • • •

Dealing with Change as an Aspiring Young Writer
by John Greig, 18

DEALING WITH CHANGE can be the most difficult challenge faced by a young writer.

Embracing change in your life or your writing is important and can influence greatly whether or not a writer chooses writing as a career. Everyone changes, sometimes quickly, sometimes slowly. And as a writer changes as a person, it is impossible that his or her writing will not be different. I struggled with changes that occurred in my life until I came to the realization that change is good for a writer. Entering high school gave me hoards of new subjects to write on.

I (so far) have found the most difficult time in my writing to be between ages 12 and 16, when I had big changes in school, body, and attitudes. I wanted to be a writer since grade two. From then until around 10 or 11 years of age, things went pretty smoothly. I wrote because I wanted to, for me, because it was fun. I could do things and explore places I could only dream of.

Then – smack – comes puberty. Suddenly romance makes a little more sense. But flying in the face of romance are gangly arms, crackling voices, and pimples. I think this is the change which decides if one wants to be a writer or not. Peer pressure becomes enormous. Writing suddenly is not cool. But it was cool for me and should be cool for you if you want it to be. Do not let anyone tell you that creating and writing are not "in." The people teenagers worship are creative writers in their own spheres. Musicians are certainly writers and poets. Because you haven't had a top 40 hit doesn't mean your writing and poetry aren't cool. Look for others who like to write. They are there in every shape and size. Maybe the captain of the hockey team, or the quiet one who sits at the back of math class slouched across her desk, or the person with the deepest voice in the school choir. Search them out. Being with other writers when your writing is changing is exciting.

And your writing will change as your body does. During the teenage years, writing is the best way to deal with the changes. Girlfriends or boyfriends, part-time jobs, sports, parties, all become great stories, so use them. This was when I stopped writing poor fantasy – my worlds were perfect, my villains were wimpy – to write about the real world and real feelings. Experiment with different styles. Read different authors. Your writing will change and eventually a voice will emerge that you will be comfortable with. Stick with that for a while, but don't be afraid to change again.

If you want a career as a writer, you must deal with change. It is the writers who can continue to write through the turbulent *and* the stable times in their lives who are successful.

● ● ● ● ●

Knowing Your Precise Skills

As a young writer, somewhere in your development (or sometime soon to come), you will have a moment when things stand still and you exclaim, "That's it! That's one thing I do really well!" In fact, you do it so well it is a unique talent.

Does your writing show that you are highly imaginative? Are your descriptions of people so sensitive that they reveal you as an alert observer of people? Does your sense of humor make people laugh?

The skills you demonstrate in your writing are one way of clueing into your own particular ability as a writer. Richard N. Bolles, a career counselor and author of *What Color is Your Parachute?*, advises people to look for work that includes their favorite skills. While thinking in terms of skills may be totally new to you, it allows you to be more inventive in both your writing and your career choices.

How many times have you heard: "You are a good writer!" "Keep on writing; you have talent." "That was a good essay." Or: "You should major in English in college, since you love to read so much." You've politely said, "Thank you," only to wonder, seconds later, what it really was that person liked about your writing.

By learning about the different skills a writer has, you can start to listen for the reason why someone is complimenting your writing.

What Do They Really Mean
When They Say...

Has anyone ever complimented your writing? What did they really mean by what they said? Read the four compliments listed below. Each is followed by a list of skills that might apply to the compliment. For each compliment you have received, choose one or two skills you think the person might have been referring to. (You may come up with skills that are not listed here.)

1. **"You are a gifted writer!"**
   - You are original in a particular area of writing (character descriptions, setting, dialogue, etc.).
   - You are able to follow detailed instructions.
   - You prioritize tasks well.
   - You complete tasks on time.
   - You see the relationship between different factors.

2. **"You wrote a wonderful story!"**
   - You are highly imaginative.
   - You are an alert observer of people.

3. "You write good letters!"
   - You express yourself well.
   - You describe people and scenes vividly.
   - You employ humor in describing experiences.
4. "You wrote a great essay!"
   - You have a memory for details.
   - You are able to compare information.
   - You communicate clearly.

In your Writer's Notebook, write down two compliments you have received in the past about your writing ability. Then write down the skills you think you were demonstrating when you were complimented.

1. Compliment: "Your story was very funny!"

   Skills: humor, character descriptions

2. Compliment: "What a story! I never expected the

   unusual ending."

   Skills: building suspense, well-thought-out plot

The next time you receive a compliment about your writing, you can use your knowledge of skills to find out what the person is really saying. If you want a clearer statement, you can prompt the person with specific questions. Here are two examples:

Reader: "I really liked your piece."
Writer: "Really? Thank you. What did you like in particular?"
Reader: "The way you described that village. I felt like I was right there."

Reader: "I really liked the way you started your story."
Writer: "That's interesting. I appreciate your saying that. What did you find pleasing about it?"
Reader: "It was a strong symbol of life, and you played upon that image until the end of the story."

"It is the moment, if you will, when a Little Leaguer
discovers, not that he or she can pitch
(which he/she may have known for some time),
but that he or she has a particular ability
to throw the good live fastball or to pop a curve
that rises or dips outrageously."

Stephen King in DANSE MACABRE

The Top Ten Basic Skills of a Writer

Out of all the skills you need to have or develop as a writer, I have compiled a list of what I think are the ten most important basic skills. They don't all have to do with the act of writing.

Think of the skills (besides writing) that you believe a good writer should have. You may want to list them in your Writer's Notebook.

Then read this list and compare it to yours.

1. Writing

You have a good sense of choosing the right words, and you use proper grammar. Your writing may show a certain flair – for humor, character descriptions, endings with twists, etc. Your writing has a unique style. You are not afraid to learn and try out new words. You are interested in how words are spelled, as well as the origins of the words you use.

2. Reading

You look for good books all the time. As you grow each year, you look for new books, perhaps award-winning books, books written by local authors, and even books written by authors in other countries. You enjoy experimenting with different types of reading.

"Read as many of the great books as you can
before the age of 22."

James Michener, author of TALES OF THE SOUTH PACIFIC,
winner of the Pulitzer Prize

3. Observation

You take the time to observe people accurately. You notice the details
of what they are wearing, how they are standing, what they are saying,
and what body language they are using. You are always noticing things,
training your eye to capture both usual and unusual items that can be
used in your settings.

"Read a lot and hit the streets.
A writer who doesn't keep up with what's out there
ain't gonna be out there."

Toni Cade Bambara, author of GORILLA, MY LOVE

4. Imagination

You have a well-developed imagination. You love to play with ideas
and events in your mind. You can create solid characters. You like to
invent scenarios in which characters are talking to each other. You can
almost see the characters right in front of you. You understand that
you can use your imagination for both fiction and nonfiction projects.

5. Project Planning

You are good at planning. You have a realistic idea of how many pages you want a writing project to be. You know your own writing habits and can plan to deliver a project on time. You understand that missing deadlines doesn't work in publishing any more than it does at school. You work effectively.

6. Research

You are able to find the facts you need – even unusual ones – to support your stories, provide the basis of a plot, and locate the best publisher. Also, you know where to look or who to ask for help in finding information.

7. Initiative

When it comes to things that are important to you, you are clear about what you want to get done, and you take steps to do it. You don't procrastinate. You identify the one person who can help you solve the problem, and you go to him or her. You find ways to get things done, even if problems keep cropping up. You don't wait for someone to tell you to do something.

"I have long since decided if you wait for the
perfect time to write, you'll never write.
There is no time that isn't flawed somehow."

Margaret Atwood, author of THE HANDMAID'S TALE

---

8. Persuasion

As a writer, you see things differently from a lot of people. Sometimes you can be ahead of your time. In order to sell a story or nonfiction book idea, you need to be able to listen to other people, yet persuade them that your project has merit. This skill can show up in your cover letter to an editor or, more importantly, a brief book proposal.

9. Typing and Word Processing

You can type over 40 words per minute. You know how to use a computer and a word processing program.

10. Financial Planning

You are able to write up your own simple budget. You are willing to learn how to set sensible financial goals and spend your money wisely. You have explored how people get paid. You have learned how writers get paid.

Rate Your Skills

You are not expected to have all ten of these skills right now or even when you graduate from high school or college. These are skills that you will acquire, work on, and refine all through your life.

Page 31 shows a page from a young writer's notebook. The writer has listed the Top Ten skills and rated his or her demonstrated ability for each one. Copy the list in your Writer's Notebook, then honestly rate yourself on these skills. A 3 can stand for "Excellent," a 2 for "Good," and a 1 for "Fair" or "Needs Work."

As you work on your writing, and as you read this book, keep in mind the skills you rated "Good" or "Fair/Needs Work." Try to come up with ways to improve in these areas. For example, financial planning may be something you do in grade 11, when you take an accounting course in school. Typing and computer skills may be scheduled for grade 9, when you start high school – or earlier, if you already use a computer.

Skill	Demonstrated Ability
1. Writing	2
2. Reading	3
3. Observing	3
4. Imagination	3
5. Project Planning	2
6. Research	1
7. Initiative	3
8. Persuasion	2
9. Typing and Word Processing	1
10. Financial Planning	1

Note to improve:

Research – ?

Typing and Word Processing – Take computer course

at school next year.

Financial Planning – Take accounting course at school

when it is offered.

READING CHALLENGE

▸ *What Color Is Your Parachute? A Practical Manual for Job Hunters and Career Changers* by Richard Nelson Bolles (Berkeley, CA: Ten Speed Press, updated annually).

This is an excellent book for students and adults who want to plan their own career path. If you have to make a career decision soon, read this book and do the exercises during a school break. If you don't have to make a career decision soon, read the introduction to this book and try to do some of the exercises.

CHAPTER THREE

Learning about Genres

EACH GENRE HAS ITS OWN particular history of development. Each genre also has its own particular set of rules. By learning about how different genres were started and have developed over the years, you can learn what type(s) of writing you do best.

In this chapter, you'll read four articles about genres by young writers. You'll learn about books to read that will make you better informed about your favorite genre(s). You'll explore where your own writing comes from, and you'll do some in-depth Writer's Notebook exercises related to genre. *Please note:* It is not my intention in this chapter to talk about specific structures or rules of different genres. There are many excellent books that do precisely that, and they are referenced in this chapter as well.

Most young writers I meet have told me they are in one of two places regarding learning about genres:

1. **They have been introduced, very briefly, to some genres (usually short stories and poetry at school), but they have never seriously considered what they would love to write.**

As Jaylene, 16, accurately put it, "I would sit down to write, and the feeling I would get was one of 'You have two choices: a) scratch off a short, disastrous poem, or b) try writing a story where you always stop in the middle of it.'"

Yet a natural part of growing up is trying out activities related to something we enjoy. For example, if you enjoy running, you will usually try out all different types of running – cross-country, hurdles, the 220-yard dash, maybe even a marathon – to see what you do best. Or you may enjoy singing, in which case you will try singing jazz, musicals, folk, rock, or opera to see what you are best at.

There is no reason in the world not to be writing your own romance or science fiction novel, if that is what you would love to do. Young writers are used to writing primarily for school assignments. It is an important switch to look at your own interests and background and consider how those could give you some clues about what you write best.

2. **They have found the genre they really love to write, but they have never learned the techniques and rules governing that genre.**

For example, a young poet realizes that the images in her poetry need to be clearer, but she has never read any poetry other than what she has been handed in school. A young adult mystery novelist knows that his plot is weak, but he has never thought of picking up a book about developing plots in mysteries. A young writer loves to write children's picture books, but he isn't aware that picture books are usually a certain number of pages in length.

For most young writers, learning more about genres is very important. Some popular genres are *fantasy, mystery, adventure, horror, romance, humor, science fiction, biography, cookbooks,* and *how-to* books. There are many more. If you are interested in the definition of a specific genre, refer to the books listed on pages 40–42.

> "Learn what you can from those you admire,
> and especially those engaged in coaching you....
> In order to be as inventive and exciting
> as a Stephane Grapelli, you have to know all your
> basic stuff first."
>
> Nigel Kennedy, British "punk" virtuoso violinist

What Four Young Writers Say about Genres

Following are four articles about genres. The views they contain are those of the young writers. The articles will give you a general sense of each genre, plus a preview of some things you should be thinking about if you are writing in that genre.

"By being surrounded by people who specialize in different genres, I learned that there is a place for all kinds of writing."

Cara, 18

● ● ● ● ●

The Picture Book

by Zahra Sachedina, 16

PICTURE BOOKS are a pleasurable yet challenging literary art form. Having become number one favorites among children, many have earned a permanent place within the heart of the young.

I can still remember myself as a young child opening up a picture book and simply adoring the myriad of colors that sprung out before me from each page! In fact, this sensation lit a spark within me, nurturing my fascination with picture books and encouraging me to focus on writing for children.

The stepping-stone that uncovered hidden talents I didn't know existed was a grade seven assignment in which I was asked to write and illustrate and hand-bind a picture book. I developed a strong sense for art as I continued creating these handmade books. Soon, I realized that my stories had begun to take shape years before I actually wrote them. They were comprised of small incidents from my child-hood; almost like photographs of memorable moments. The secret to good writing had been unlocked...writing about what I know best.

Many young authors overlook this genre, as it is not as well recognized as poetry writing or short story writing. The following guidelines may be considered when writing picture books:

1. Begin by choosing an age group you wish to write for. Follow this age guide to help you put your story into perspective.

2. Explore your genre fully, that is, read what other picture book authors have written to gain a solid foundation.

3. Write and edit a rough draft. Have someone else read it for a second opinion.

4. If you wish to illustrate your story, plan your pictures and text on a storyboard before you start the actual illustrations.

5. Transfer the storyboard ideas onto your final copy and complete it with detailed illustrations. You may wish to bind the book for a professional finish.

One of the main things to remember is that the book should be read *aloud*, and therefore try to develop a rhythm/rhyme scheme throughout the story in order to maintain a sense of oral imagery.

● ● ● ● ●

• • • • •

Playwriting

by Angie Kays, 17

OFTEN PLAYWRITING IS OVERLOOKED as a possible genre for young writers. As you look over your own writing, there are clues that suggest a possible strength for writing drama. Does your dialogue run on for pages and pages in a seemingly endless flow? Do you attach more importance to what your characters say and how they say it than to any other element of your stories? Do your descriptions of settings and characters' actions read like stage directions? When you write, do you visualize your work being performed?

Through my experience of having my plays "workshopped" (produced on stage and directed with professional help), I have learned a lot about writing plays. For example:

1. **Always be listening.** In restaurants, on buses, constantly listen so that natural dialogue seeps into your subconsciousness and then pours out freely in your writing. Observe people, not only for what they say, but also for what they don't say. Often theater is the motion behind the thought; it's the equivalent of reading between the lines in literature.

2. **Use an outline.** Dialogue has a funny way of getting stuck in one place. A plot outline helps keep dialogue flowing smoothly and advancing through the beginning, middle, and end of your piece.

3. **Keep your characters distinct.** Give each one a unique vocabulary and a favorite expression. Just as all of us have different speech patterns in real life, characters in plays should as well.

Finally, *read*. Read Chekhov, Aristophanes, Moliere, and Fennario. Devour the imagery of Shakespeare. Most of all, never ever stifle the conversations that go on in your head. They can be some of the most powerful material for your plays!

• • • • •

• • • • •

Writing for the Children's Market: Children Ages 8–12
by Jaylene Rashleigh, 16

I CAME WITH THE IDEA that I wrote for young adults and no one else. As it turns out, I'm also interested in children's books. I suppose the fact that I really like working with primary children and watching them learn has brought this fact out. I had never really thought about writing children's books.

Your imagination really has no limits to what you wish to write or how you wish to present it. If you are lucky enough to be near children, as I am, the situations you are pulled into with them are usually rich in ideas and plots. And you can find stories in everyday routines or situations: baby-sitting, tutoring, or even talking with your siblings.

What qualities should a young writer writing children's novels possess?

- A natural ability to understand how children think, feel, and act in certain situations.

- The ability to write stories from a child's point of view.

- An understanding that younger children have a different vocabulary. For example, children, age eight, rarely talk about a tax budget. They are concerned, though, about how much the candy at the corner is going to cost and if they have enough money.

- Knowing what children fear. For example, the first jump off a diving board or being submerged in water.

If you wish to write for children, get yourself into contact with them and find out what they are really like. Never be afraid to try your ideas out on them; seeing their initial reaction can aid you greatly.

• • • • •

• • • • •

Writing Poetry
by Jess Perlitz, 15

To ME, WRITING POETRY is not only a way of expressing myself and a type of therapy, but a way to draw others into my own world. I'm not sure what it is that I like about poetry more than prose. It could be the ability to create feelings that the reader may have never felt, to induce thought not yet having been labeled, or the ability to construct a whole new universe through which poetry allows me to travel. It could also be the surreal freedom I feel when writing poetry, or the lack of guidelines that I feel I have to follow. It feels strange for me to be giving advice on poetry when to me it is still a whole world that I have begun to explore.

In my mind, the most important thing when writing is to write for yourself and to make use of the freedom that poetry allows as effectively as possible. The power of poetry can be remarkable. All you need is paper, pen, and a mind needing freedom. If it is for therapy that you are writing, then let your feelings drip; if it is to make a statement – be bold. Poetry has no definite shape. The body and mind of poetry is only what you make it.

• • • • •

Reading to Become Informed about Your Favorite Genres

There are two types of reading you can do to develop confidence in the genres you are writing in (or want to write in):

1. **You can read all the good books in the genres you are interested in.** This gives you an invaluable background. If you are interested in writing young adult adventures, read the books that are classics and/or have won awards or prizes.

2. **You can read some of the how-to books and critical essays about your chosen genres.** Develop a sense of the rules that can and can't be broken.

I call this step in a young writer's development "gathering vital background information." It is a fundamental step for any writer, young or old, who wishes to get published. Experience has shown that young writers who are clear about the rules and background behind genres are much more confident about their writing and produce writing of a higher quality.

Following is a short list of recommended books on various genres. They are fun to read and fun to work through, especially as you can work through them at your own pace. If you find some of them too long to read at first (some are 150–200 pages), don't be discouraged. Read through the Table of Contents and see if there are particular chapters that are of interest to you. Skim the index and look for topics that catch your eye. Or flip through the book and watch for headings or graphics that make you want to know more. You don't have to read the whole book at once. You might read one part one day, then set the book aside to pick up again at a later date.

For books about other types of genres – mystery, romance, comedy, etc. – ask your librarian or media specialist, check the writing section in your local bookstore, or write to: Writer's Digest Books, 1507 Dana Avenue, Cincinnati, OH 45207, U.S.A.

You might also find it helpful and inspiring to read books by (and about) writers who talk about their craft in more personal, autobiographical terms. For a few suggestions, see pages 160–161.

Animated Films and Puppets

- *Disney's Aladdin: The Making of an Animated Film* by John Culhane (New York: Hyperion, 1992).

- *Jim Henson: The Works: The Art, The Magic, The Imagination* by Christopher Finch (New York: Random House, 1993).

Children's Picture Books

- *Draw and Write Your Own Picture Book* by Emily Hearn and Mark Thurman (Richmond Hill: Pembroke, 1989). This book was specifically written for the young writer. It is very easy to read (32 pages) and work with.

- *Drawing with Children: A Creative Teaching and Learning Method that Works for Adults, Too* by Mona Brookes (Los Angeles: Jeremy P. Tarcher, 1986). To all those writers whose drawing consists of stick people, the good news is: There is hope! Here is a relatively simple method for dramatically improving anyone's drawing ability.

- *How to Plan Your Drawings* by Mark Thurman (Markham: Pembroke, 1992). Another 32-page book written for the young writer/illustrator, full of simple procedures that help bring characters and stories to life.

- *How to Write and Sell Children's Picture Books* by Jean E. Karl (Cincinnati, OH: Writer's Digest Books, 1994).

- *Writing Picture Books: What Works and What Doesn't* by Kathy Stinson (Markham: Pembroke, 1991). Describes the vital steps of writing texts for picture books.

- *Writing Your Best Picture Book Ever* by Kathy Stinson, illustrations by Alan and Lea Daniel (Markham: Pembroke, 1994).

Film and Television

- *Burton on Burton,* edited by Mark Salisbury (London: Faber, 1995). Tim Burton, one of the great visionaries of contemporary filmmaking (*Batman, Beetlejuice, Pee Wee's Big Adventure, Edward Scissorhands, The Nightmare Before Christmas*), discusses his work.

- *Potter on Potter,* edited by Graham Fuller (London: Faber, 1993). Dennis Potter, one of television's best dramatists ("Pennies from Heaven," "The Singing Detective"), discusses his work.

Horror and Fantasy

- *Danse Macabre* by Stephen King (New York: Berkeley Publishing Group, 1985). The best-selling horror writer traces the development of the genre from 1930 to 1980.

- *How to Write Tales of Horror, Fantasy, and Science Fiction* by J.N. Williamson (Cincinnati, OH: Writer's Digest Books, 1991).

Nonfiction

- *Nonfiction for Children: How to Write It, How to Sell It* by Ellen E.M. Roberts (Cincinnati: Writer's Digest Books, 1986).

Novel

- *Guide to Fiction Writing,* 2nd edition, by Phyllis A. Whitney (Boston: The Writer, 1988).
- *The Complete Guide to Writing Fiction* by Barnaby Conrad (Cincinnati, OH: Writer's Digest Books, 1990).

Poetry

- *The Universe Is One Poem: Four Poets Talk about Poetry,* edited by George Swede (Toronto: Simon & Pierre, 1990).

Romance

- *The Craft of Writing Romance* by J. Saunders (London: Allison and Busy, 1986).
- *How to Write Romances* by Phyllis Taylor Pianka (Cincinnati: Writer's Digest Books, 1988).

Short Story (for Adults and Children)

- *Writing for Children and Teenagers,* 3rd edition, by Lee Wyndham and Arnold Madison (Cincinnati, OH: Writer's Digest Books, 1988).
- *Writing the Short Story: A Hands-On Writing Program* by Jack M. Bickham (Cincinnati, OH: Writer's Digest Books, 1994).

Young Adult Novel

- *Writing Young Adult Novels* by Hadley Irwin and Jeannette Eyerly (Cincinnati, OH: Writer's Digest Books, 1987).

Knowing Where Your Writing Comes From

You can use any technique or method to locate your interests and background. Here are five areas you can look at in your life, to see if they might play a part in your future writing.

1. Your Favorite Projects

This category is not limited to projects you did at school. You may have done a community project with a group you belong to. You may have done a project with your family. You may have done something entirely by yourself as a hobby.

These projects could indicate your interest in a particular type of writing. For example, I'll never forget the shock I had one day when I realized that my first book (a series of mini-biographies of famous Canadians) was almost an exact replica of a school project I did in elementary school on famous people.

You may find that you have always enjoyed writing poetry but have had trouble with short-story assignments. Or you may have loved writing a history project because it was about a period of time that fascinated you. Your interest in that period could be turned into research for a historical novel, or even a thriller with flashbacks to that period in time.

"The selection of a theme is never an accident with any writer; its provenance, however, does sometimes seem to be thrown in one's way like a coin in the sand, which catches the light when one walks past at a certain angle."

Mary Renault, author of THE BULL FROM THE SEA

2. Your Favorite Books

A survey of your favorite authors can uncover the genres you prefer to write in. For example, if J.R.R. Tolkien and Terry Pratchett are on your list, you may have a natural interest in writing fantasy. If you appreciate the works of Alice Munro or O'Henry, you may have an interest in short stories. An interest in Margaret Laurence, Albert Camus, and Pat Conroy may indicate a desire to write full-length novels.

You may read some books simply to "escape." Many people find mysteries the most wonderful books to relax with. Other books may be a challenge, but not related to a genre you're interested in writing in. You read them because you want to read them.

3. Your Interests

Your interests can indicate your own writing angle or the particular audience you intend to write for. For example, if you have a strong interest in science, you may write science fiction, science textbooks, or essays on science (as do Lewis Thomas, Annie Dillard, Stephen J. Gould, and Carl Sagan). If you work with young children, perhaps teaching swimming, you may find that you have a natural ability to tell stories and hold the interest of children. The hero in your story may be a swimming instructor! If you have an interest in law and plan to become a lawyer, you may end up writing legal thrillers in your spare time (like John Grisham).

4. Your Writing Skills

Do your writing skills show a tendency for you to write pieces of a particular length? For example, if you are already writing long stories (100 pages or more), you may be a natural candidate for writing novels. Or how about your school assignments? Do you get so involved in the complexities of a history essay that you write twice the word limit? You may be a natural nonfiction book or article writer.

5. Your Family and Community

Just as some people get handed down the family business, you may find that your family (and the community you live in) give you great ideas you can use in your writing. For example, your great-aunt may tell you how she worked on radar in World War II, which you can turn into the background of a play. Or your next-door neighbor may love electronics and pass along some information to you that ends up in a science fiction short story.

• • •

The point is, outside influences can have a profound effect on your writing. If you let your everyday activities, natural interests, and what brings you joy guide you, your writing can only deepen in scope.

"I don't choose my stories, they choose me.
Things come to my mind. Sometimes it takes
years and years for them to coalesce –
it's like iron filings collecting on a magnet."

Katherine Anne Porter, winner of the Pulitzer Prize
for her COLLECTED SHORT STORIES

Where Does Your Writing Come From?

In your Writer's Notebook, write at least *two* responses to each of the following questions:

1. What are two projects (at school, in a club, in your community, or at home) that you enjoy doing (or have enjoyed doing) the most?

2. Who are your favorite authors?

3. What are your main interests?

4. What are your best writing skills? (Take these from the work you did for "Writer's Notebook: What Do They Really Mean When They Say…" on pages 25-27.)

5. What fields or occupations have your relatives been employed in?

Now think about your responses. Are there any clues that you might be interested in a type of writing you haven't tried? Are there two or three genres you think you may now be attracted to? List them in your Writer's Notebook for future reference.

Writing What You Write Best

This exercise will take some time and effort on your part, but the rewards you reap will be tremendous. It is divided into two "plans." Select the one that best fits where you are at the present time. Adapt it to suit your needs where necessary.

- **Plan One** is for young writers who have not really had a chance to explore other genres. For example, you may have been selecting genres such as short stories or poetry because you have been asked to write these for school. If you write short stories because you can end them when you run out of steam, or if you keep writing poems because you have no idea how to write anything longer, it is time to look around and explore whether you have a natural talent for any other genre.

- **Plan Two** is for writers who know which genre they love and want to know more about its rules and structures. For example, you have written a mystery short story, but you don't know what the rules of the genre are. Or you have written a romance novel, but you don't feel that your main character is as good as he or she could be.

Plan One

Start by determining three different genres that interest you right now. Write these in your Writer's Notebook. Then follow these steps, moving at your own pace.

Step 1: For each genre that interests you, select a book from the recommended reading list on pages 40–42. (If you can't find the titles listed here, check your local library or school media center for other books on those genres.)

Step 2: Read at least one book from each genre that has won an award. Your librarian can help you find these.

In your Writer's Notebook, record the steps as you take them, perhaps along with a few notes on ideas and results from your reading. Move on to Plan Two when you feel ready.

PETER'S PLAN

Three genres I am interested in:

   1. Adult Novels

   2. Young Adult Novels

   3. Mystery Short Stories for Children

Step 1: I will read the chapters I find interesting in one book

on structure for each genre:

   1. Guide to Fiction Writing

   2. Writing for Children and Teenagers

   3. How to Write Short Stories for Young People

Step 2: I will read one award-winning book from each genre:

   1. Ask librarian about winner of Booker Prize.

   2. Read Dragon Fall by Lee J. Hindle.

   3. Ask librarian about mystery award winners.

Plan Two

If you have found the genre you really love to write in, or if you have completed Plan One and feel ready to go further, follow this plan.

In your Writer's Notebook, write down one or two genres that you will focus on. Then follow these steps, moving at your own pace.

Step 1: Read in depth one or more books on the structure of your preferred genre.

Step 2: Read at least three books in your genre that have won awards, preferably by different authors and, if possible, by authors of different nationalities and ethnic or cultural backgrounds.

Take all the time you need to complete these two steps. They may take you two weeks, or they may take you six months, depending on your schedule. Once again, record your progress and any comments in your Writer's Notebook.

Working on one or two genres with an understanding of how each one really works, rather than dabbling all over the place with no clear idea of what you are doing, helps to build your confidence as a writer. Remember Cinderella, who just naturally slipped into that slipper? That is the sort of fit you want. Somewhere along the line, writers have made decisions about what genres they want to work in – for a particular book, for a year, or for the rest of their lives. Then they have sat down and started to write.

CHRISTINE'S PLAN

Genres I will focus on:

    1. Children's picture books (ages 6–9)

    2. Children's novels (ages 8–12)

Step 1: I will read in depth one or more books on structure.

    1. <u>The Children's Picture Book</u>

    2. <u>Writing for Children and Teenagers</u>

Step 2: I will read at least 3 books:

Children's Picture Books (ages 6–9)

    1. <u>The Paperbag Princess</u> by Bob Munsch

    2. <u>Madeleine</u> by Ludwig Bemelmans

    3. <u>The Snowy Day</u> by Ezra Jack Keats

Children's Novels (ages 8–12)

    1. <u>Mama's Going to Buy You a Mockingbird</u> by Jean Little

    2. <u>The Jungle Book</u> by Rudyard Kipling

    3. <u>Matilda</u> by Roald Dahl

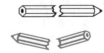

A Day in the Life

This exercise is for young writers who want to try their hand at either creating a mini-biography (1,500 words) or a historical short story (2,000 words). For the young writer interested in being published, either of these could be used in an educational anthology. (You are probably familiar with educational anthologies. They are used in English classes. They contain poems, stories, etc. by a variety of authors. One young writer, who recently won a Prism Award for her short story, had it published in an educational anthology in Canada.)

This exercise allows you to focus on a particular day in a famous person's life and create a setting and mood based on information from a variety of new sources. Along the way, you strengthen your skills in researching for unusual facts and building your imagination. As you develop scenes for different times in history, you learn to improve the settings, mood, and atmosphere of your writing.

First, you need to decide what famous person you want to write about. Is there anyone in particular who interests you? Anyone you would like to learn more about? Anyone whose life and times you would like to explore? (If you get an assignment to write about a specific person, you won't be able to choose your subject. But you can still use this exercise to make the assignment more interesting and fun.)

Next, you need to pick one day in that person's life to write about. This can be any day:

- a birthday
- the day he invented or discovered something
- the day before she invented or discovered something
- the day he met a special friend

- her first day of school
- an event that scared him
- or...?

Creating good biographies and historical fiction is a combination of finding interesting facts, placing yourself in a particular time, and finding an "angle" – a way to make your writing unique.

Finding Interesting Facts

Where can you go to find really interesting facts? Here are some suggestions:

- **Unusual dictionaries.** You'll find all kind of dictionaries (including books and CD-ROMs) in your local library or school media center. There are dictionaries of slang, music, art, science, science fiction, mythology, superstitions, symbols, and just about anything else you can possibly imagine.

- **Books about a country's customs.** These books will give you information about national holidays, ethnic festivals, games, festival foods, why certain holidays occur, how certain holidays are celebrated, and more. If you would like to learn more about special days and how they might apply to a person chosen for this project, I recommend:
  - *Let's Celebrate* by Carolyn Parry (Toronto: Kids Can Press, 1987)
  - *The American Book of Days* by Jane M. Hatch (New York: H.W. Wilson Co., 1978)
  - *Writing Down the Days* by Lorraine M. Dalhstrom (Minneapolis: Free Spirit Publishing, 1990).

- **History books.** These may answer questions about what people were wearing, what they were eating, the types of newspapers or books they were reading, unusual community laws, etc. For example, while I was researching my book, *Madeleine de Vercheres*, I came across a whole set of city laws. I learned that in the early 1700s in the city of Montreal, one law said that if you owned a dog, it needed to be in the house by 9:00 p.m. That fact alone could be the basis of an interesting children's story.

- **Geography books.** These may answer questions about a favorite place your subject might have visited, the climate at a particular time of year, the surroundings of a person's house, etc.

- **Journals, diaries, or books of letters.** These may reveal a subject's personal thoughts about people in his or her life, what his or her home looked like, and a favorite pet. For example, while I was researching books to write a short biography of Lucy Maud Montgomery, I found her journals to be a wonderful source of material regarding childhood superstitions and special occasions at school. One superstition was that if a young woman counted nine stars for nine nights, the first boy she shook hands with would be her future husband!

Placing Yourself in a Particular Time

You've chosen a famous person to write about, and you've picked a day in his or her life to focus on. You've used a variety of resources to find interesting facts about the person's life and times. Now you need to do some "time traveling." You need to imagine what it would really be like to live when that person lived. Questions like these can get you started:

- What might she have been reading that day? (Books? Newspapers? Magazines? What reading materials were available?)

- What type of music might he have been listening to?

- If she went to work, how did she get there?

- What clothes could he have worn?

- If she went to school, what might the school have looked like?

- What might have made him happy or sad on that day?

- What was her family like?

- Did he have a close relationship with anyone in particular?

- Did she have a pet?

You probably know some or all of the answers already from your research. If not, you may want to research some more. The answers can be woven into your mini-biography or short story.

Finding a Particular "Angle"

Authors of biography and historical fiction bring their own individual angles to a subject. Because of this, no two biographies or pieces of historical fiction are the same.

You will want to leave your own individual imprint. For example, you may choose to write more about the famous person's family, or you may choose to write about the thoughts he or she was having while creating an invention, or you may choose to focus on the problems he or she had to overcome as a child or teenager.

Writing...and Beyond

You should be ready now to write a mini-biography or a historical short story of 1,500–2,000 words. When you finish writing, show your biography or short story to a friend. If you really like what you have written, why not try to get it published? See Chapter Five for suggestions.

As an option, if you wrote a mini-biography, why not try writing a short story from the same research? You may learn something interesting!

CHAPTER FOUR

Playing with Your Imagination

WHEN YOU WALK DOWN THE STREET, when you sit in school, and when you see a movie, you are making up your mind about what you like. What you find pleasing to look at or to do reflects your tastes and your viewpoints. You can bring your own joy, tastes, and viewpoints to your stories, poems, or articles.

Have you ever stopped to think why people are attracted to different things? Why your mother may think that looking at the sunset beats seeing any movie? Why your brother loves photography, but you prefer writing? Young writers put their own signature on the words they choose and the way they arrange them. Give yourself the time to let your imagination soar.

Four Ways to Keep Track of Your Ideas

1. Favorite Passages File Folders

Oftentimes you may be reading and find yourself saying, "That was a really great piece of writing." You then flip the page and keep going. Next time, why not mark the page with a Post-it note or paper clip, then jot down the passage later to slip into a favorite passages file folder? (You can also use a box of 3" × 5" cards organized by topic.) The passages you write down may strike a particular chord one day when you need inspiration for a writing project. Watch for spectacular settings, vivid character descriptions, first encounters, or anything that really strikes you.

Here are two of my favorites:

- An exquisite scene of a boy trying to get close enough to give his first-ever kiss is found in *Daniel Martin,* a novel by John Fowles. It goes on for pages and ends with these lines: "She just stopped and turned, so abruptly that he almost bumped into her; put her hands and the flowers behind her back and simply stared at him, the old game of staring. Five seconds it lasted. Then she closed her eyes and raised her mouth to be kissed. He hesitated, he poised, he somehow found his hands gingerly on her upper arms; then the entire world, or sixteen years of it, melted."

- In *Madame Bovary,* Gustave Flaubert immortalizes a sound: "The stones striking the wooden coffin made that awesome sound which seems to us the reverberation of eternity."

2. Diaries

Most writers keep a personal diary or journal. How can these help your writing? It really is up to you and the type of records you keep. On one hand, the practice keeps your observational powers sharp. On the other hand, you may have an ongoing question about a problem or a person, and recording your thoughts and answers may turn out to be very useful for the basis of a scene or a story. With a very long-term view, you can always use your teenage diaries as research for when you are an adult and looking to write a young adult novel!

Personal diaries are a wonderful way to keep track of your ideas and views. I still have the diaries I wrote as a teenager. I only wish I had kept slightly more interesting ones. In looking back at my diaries, I seem to have been in the habit of recording all the day-to-day events of my life. Also, I seem to have been fascinated by tracking NHL hockey games and my tennis scores!

"There is nothing too trifling to write down....
You will be surprised to find on re-perusing
your journal what an importance and graphic power
these little particulars assume."

Nathaniel Hawthorne, author of THE SCARLET LETTER

3. Image Journals

This idea for another type of journal was brought to my attention by a media arts student who helped at my first writers' camp.

An image journal is made up of both writing and illustrations. The illustrations can range from photographs you have taken, to clippings cut from magazines, to postcards, cartoons, etc. The writing can be your own writing, quotations you like, and/or words or paragraphs from books or articles you have read.

An image journal is a fun way to record ideas and images that interest you, and that you can later use for your own writing. A photo of a red-haired girl inspired Lucy Maud Montgomery to write *Anne of Green Gables*.

Use any blank or lined book you like. You can buy any kind at a stationery store or bookstore. It is best to use a book that is at least 8½" × 11", since this will give you room for large pictures. You can also use a loose-leaf binder or photo album so you can insert pages and move them around as you please. You may even find that index cards make good mounts for pictures.

Under each image, write something about it. Why do you like it? What appeals to you? Does it remind you of something? Is there a story or poem behind it? You can keep an image journal for a fantasy, a mystery, or any type of story. For example, you might want to collect pictures of all sorts of unusual characters from comics and magazines to give you ideas for characters in your fantasy stories. Or cut photos out of magazines for scenes in a mystery. Do you get the idea?

It's also fun to collect images from a particular focus. This is especially helpful if you live in a country where a particular type of animal or plant is not found. If you collect close-ups, it's almost as good as being there!

4. Special Journals

You can keep any type of journal you like, depending on your writing interests. My friend, Catriona, was working on her first novel and wanted to make sure that she was accurately recording the seasons in England. She found it useful to keep a weather diary, where she recorded everything from the first spring flowers to the patterns of thunderstorms. She found using a small desk diary useful. Here is one of Catriona's entries:

June 1. Another scorching summer day to begin June. Phillip actually got his first case of sunburn. Peonies out. Also some small blue-and-yellow irises. Horse chestnuts in flower: notice variety of color.

Making Time to Write

Professional writers have been writing for so long that they have figured out the best time of day to work, as well as what keeps them writing. I know some writers, including myself, who realize that when we are writing full-time, it is not unusual for us to put in an 11-hour day. And then there are other writers who work only half the day, either in the morning or afternoon.

We use all sorts of individually quirky habits to keep us sane while we are writing intensely. For example, only when I am writing (and when I've finished directing a writers' camp) do I eat doughnuts! My breaks include everything from swimming to jogging, to simply sitting outside and letting the brain cells solve a problem, to reading a quick one-hour mystery. I know exactly how long I need off and how to keep my brain sharp. At the end of a book, I usually take a week's holiday somewhere sunny to turn my brain cells into "off" mode and give them a chance to recover.

Other authors use other techniques or habits. The point is that over the years, we've each developed a discipline that will produce a manuscript *no matter what.*

"Every morning between 9 and 12 I go to my room and sit before a piece of paper. Many times I just sit for three hours with no ideas coming to me. But I know one thing: If an idea does come between 9 and 12, I am there ready for it."

Flannery O'Connor, author of
EVERYTHING THAT RISES MUST CONVERGE

I have seen the most extraordinary results from the young writers I have worked with who got over their obstacles and designed a writing schedule. Second drafts of full-length novels, a runner-up award (and eventual first prize) in the National Written & Illustrated By...Awards Contest for Students, poetry awards, etc., etc., have all been the result of the young writers applying themselves more consistently to their work. They took their talent more seriously and went on to develop their own individual disciplines.

The only way to learn what works for you in your writing life is to make the time to write. The more you write, the more you will see of your own writing style. Thoughts you didn't even know you had will take shape on the paper or computer screen. Character sketches will turn into full-dimensional characters with strong internal motives and a past history, as well as hair, eyes, teeth, and personality.

If you want to write well, you need to put time aside to learn the craft. It helps to schedule a regular time, because you will set up an important discipline for later in life. You will train yourself to sit down and write, whether you need to or want to.

Tip: If you need help releasing yourself from endless hours of school work (and to prepare wisely if you are going to college), you may want to read *Use Your Head* by Tony Buzan (see page 85). This book helps you process information at high speeds, organize projects more effectively, bring out your individual creativity, and as a result get higher marks. In England, where university clubs have been formed around this book, students are earning some of the highest marks in their classes!

Your regular writing time can be as long or short as you want, depending on your writing aspirations.

"The history of literature is the history of prolific people. I always say to students, give me four pages a day, *every* day."

Ray Bradbury, author of FAHRENHEIT 451

When You Write Best

There are probably more views about when to write than on any other topic in writing. Some people write only when they feel like it; others can't afford to be so free and easy, so they sort out a regular routine.

Try out different parts of the day until you find your best time. Also, think about where you are when you come up with some of your best ideas. I've often been caught on the stairs with the brilliant flash of a whole outline of a book, and I had to sit down and write it right there on the steps. (As a result, I am rarely without paper and pen wherever I go – even if it means stuffing them into my jeans pockets.)

"When I am...completely myself, entirely alone... or during the night when I cannot sleep, it is on such occasions that my ideas flow best and most abundantly. Whence and how these come I know not nor can I force them...."

Wolfgang Amadeus Mozart, composer

Three Case Studies from a Young Writers' Club

1. Dave, 14

The problem: Dave found that he got inspired by an idea, then his interest would drop off. His excuse for stopping: "I lost interest in the plot."

The solution: After some discussion, Dave started to look at what exactly he was trying to write. Once he had decided it was a short story, rather than just some free form with no direction, he structured a plot outline and found he could finish his original idea.

2. Shane, 17

The problem: Shane found that on some nights he could write, but on others he just couldn't seem to control the idea flow. His excuse for stopping: "No inspiration."

The solution: The whole idea of writing even when he was supposedly "uninspired" was new to Shane. He put a certain amount of time aside every week and began to write no matter what he felt like. In fact, he commented later that it was a little like getting into homework. Once he was into it, he was fine. But sitting down and getting to work sometimes took more effort.

"I don't know exactly where ideas come from, but when I'm working well ideas just appear."

Jim Henson, creator of the Muppets

3. Sharon, 13

The problem: Sharon started off great. She wrote for five days in a row, for an average of 800–900 words per day. Then she slipped to 200 words. Then she stopped. Her excuse for stopping: "Ran out of time."

The solution: Sharon was in the eighth grade and unused to scheduling an activity for longer than a week. She got a year's calendar and started to schedule her writing for one complete school term. Sharon had been used to attending tennis lessons once a week, but this was scheduled by her parents. It was a new idea for her to schedule her writing hobby herself.

"I don't wait for moods. You accomplish nothing if you do that. Your mind must know it has got to get down to work."

Pearl S. Buck, author of THE GOOD EARTH,
winner of the Pulitzer Prize and the Nobel Prize for Literature

In each case, the young writer made a commitment to write, ran into an obstacle, and then came up with a solution. Some obstacles were caused by simply having to fit something new into an already busy homework and social schedule. Others were caused by plotting problems, a lack of clarity regarding genre, or a poorly defined character.

"Nature rarely speaks.
Hence the whirlwind does not last a whole morning,
Nor the sudden rainstorm last a whole day.
What causes these?
Heaven and Earth.
If Heaven and Earth cannot make them long lasting,
How much less so can humans?"

THE TAO OF POWER, translation of TAO TE CHING by R.L. Wing

How to Schedule Your Writing: Divide and Conquer

It helps when you are planning to do any piece of writing to have an idea of the number of pages it will be and how long you want the writing to take you.

Unless you have entered contests that require a specific word count, the notion of thinking how many pages your piece will have may be totally new to you. Yet if you ask any author who is currently working on a writing project for adults how long his book will be, he or she can likely give you a very good idea. If you ask an author who is working on a picture book for children, he or she will give you an *exact* number of pages, based on the age group he or she is writing for.

Estimating page counts is something that comes with practice. But it is also a valuable tool in training you to see the finished book or short story. For those of you who never seem to finish a short story or novel, this might be an interesting thought to consider.

One year in my private consulting, I had the pleasure of working with a boy named Aric who was in the seventh grade and had always wanted to write a horror novel. Previously, he had only written short stories, usually ten pages long (2,500 words). He wrote them when he felt like it.

Aric decided to try writing a 100-page young adult novel. The whole notion of scheduling was new to him, so we worked out a schedule together. To sort out his schedule, he did the following calculations:

Step 1: He figured out how many words were on a typewritten double-spaced page. He came up with 250 words per page (which is fairly standard).

Step 2: He multiplied 100 pages × 250 words per page and learned that he would be writing 25,000 words.

Step 3: He looked at how long it had taken him in the past to write a short story of 2,500 words. He figured one week of writing for a total of five hours. If it took 1 week to write 10 pages, then it would take 10 weeks to write 100 pages. Obviously that didn't include detailed character sketches or plot outlines, but Aric could use it as a rough guide.

Step 4: He marked off his calendar and assigned a chapter for each week. Then he got to work!

You don't need to use quite the same method that Aric did. You can adapt it to suit your own needs. But it really helps to set a realistic schedule for getting a written piece finished.

Making a Timetable

There are two parts to this exercise. In the first part, you see what your current writing habits are. In the second part, you get a sense of a schedule for a current writing project.

Part 1

Following are some questions you need to answer to determine your current writing habits. Start a fresh page in your Writer's Notebook.

1. How much time do you spend writing?

2. How much time in a typical week do you actually have free to write? How many hours do you actually spend writing? What is the ratio of free time to time spent writing?

3. Are you writing as much as you want to during a typical week? If your answer is "yes," go on to Part 2.

4. If your answer is "no," how many hours or how many words do you want to write a week?

5. What would you have to do to make this work? (For example, do you find it easier to schedule major writing periods during a summer vacation or winter or spring break?)

Part 2

Now take a look at a writing project you would like to start or are currently working on. How will you schedule it? How will you plan your time so you are sure to get it done? Here's an example of one way to do this.

Marlene, age 16, receives the October issue of her favorite magazine and notices the rules for a short story contest. She decides to write a 2,000-word short story for the contest. To help her organize her time, she uses these calculations:

1. The length of the piece = 2,000 words.
2. 2,000 words divided by 250 words (the number of words on a double-spaced typewritten page) = 8 pages.
3. The number of hours a week available for writing: 4 hours.
4. The number of weeks before the contest deadline: 5 weeks.
5. 4 hours every 5 weeks = 20 hours to finish short story.
6. 2,000 words divided by 20 hours = 100 words/hour.

This gives Marlene a realistic idea of how many words she needs to write each hour she sits down to write. Obviously, on some days she may write more and some days she may write less, but she has a realistic target. This also helps her when planning her plot outline. She has a good idea of how long each segment of her story needs to be. Marlene prepares this timetable to keep herself on schedule:

```
Marlene's Timetable

Mon.   Tues.   Wed.   Thurs.   Fri.   Sat.   Sun.

                1       1               1      1

Total Hours Per Week = 4
```

Study Marlene's estimated project time and word count. Now figure out your own estimates for your writing project and record them in your Writer's Notebook.

You can also use a timetable like this for much longer projects, such as young adult novels which require 125–250 pages. Or, if you like to write and illustrate your own books, you can plan your drawing and

writing time and submit your piece for the National Written &
Illustrated By…Awards Contest for Students sponsored annually by
Landmark Editions (see page 96). You can also use this method very
successfully for school projects.

Feel free to modify this timetable to work for you. Each writer has
unique habits and schedules that work for him or her. Make sure that
you are giving yourself enough time to write the best piece possible –
and to complete it in time to submit it to a contest or publisher.

Make a chart outlining the time you want to spend writing each
day and each week. Total the hours to see if this is the amount of time
you were hoping for. Are you surprised by the amount? Think about
your other activities and decide if there is anything you do that is less
important to you than your writing. Set aside some of this time for
writing. You may find that a daily or weekly calendar is an easier way
to schedule and track your writing time.

Two Ways to Organize Your Writing

1. Outlines

You have probably learned some types of outlines at school – either in
answering questions for an English test, or in following a simple plot
outline for a writing assignment.

In outlining a short story or novel, writers use all sorts of meth-
ods. Some use a visual aid (a storyboard), some use a verbal aid (a plot
outline or a one-paragraph synopsis of the action of the whole book),
some use a combination of the two, and some just get a vague outline
in their head. The point is not to argue about which method is best,
because obviously all writers have their own method. The point is,
what do *you* do as a young writer when your story has unexpectedly
come to a stop and you can't seem to bring it back to life?

One thing you *can* do is try the Plot Breakdown Repair Kit
described on pages 68–69. You can also look for more books that give
suggestions about how to fix your plot or get control of your plot

when problems arise. You'll find a list of books on pages 40–42. Or go to the library and look for books on your genre. You are not the first writer to face these problems! Other writers have figured out ways to solve them, and some of their ideas might work for you, too.

2. Storyboards

A storyboard is wonderful way to organize your thoughts for fiction or nonfiction writing. It provides a visual outline of where you are going.

Storyboards are most commonly used for picture books as a way to draw the story first and then write in the words. Nonfiction writers and novel writers can use them as visual aids for chapters. I use them because I am very concerned with how my nonfiction books are designed. I keep a sense of what each double-page spread looks like in my head so I know the reader can read the book easily and have fun with it. It is not unusual to find one whole wall of my writing room plastered with current chapter outlines and storyboards.

You can make your own storyboard simply by drawing the same number of squares as the pages of the article, book, or play you are working on. Use blank paper, and keep a master so you can photocopy it easily, rather than making a new storyboard each time you want to write something.

Storyboards have long been common in advertising for designing commercials and other audio-visual materials, and by television and movie studios for creating storylines and animated films. But the type of storyboard I use is slightly different. It was designed by Canadian author and illustrator Mark Thurman (best known for the comic, "Mighty Mites"), who developed it to teach young people how to write and illustrate fiction picture books. Given my love of nonfiction books, I asked Mark's permission to use his storyboards in my workshops on coaching nonfiction as well as fiction. An example of a first draft of a 24-page storyboard completed by two young writers – a 10-year-old and an 11-year-old – is shown on pages 66–67.

**24 PAGE
STORY BOARD**

FRONT COVER

INSIDE/FRONT COVER

**The World of
Bears**
by Lauren and
Victoria

(1)
This book is
based on the
spectacled
bears at Jersey
Zoo.

(6)
Every two years
the mother bear
has twins.

(7)
—

(8)
The father is
two times bigger
than the mother
bear.

(9)
—

(14)
The father bear
might not like
his own cubs and
they might have
a fight.

(15)
—

(16)
And if they do
the cubs will be
sent to another
zoo.

(17)
—

(22)
A suitable zoo
will be selected

(23)
—

(24)
and one of the
bears will get
taken to it.

INSIDE/BACK COVER

(2)
The bears are
called specta-
cled bears
because of the
brown ring
around their
eyes.

(3)
— .

(4)
They are wild
creatures and
are mostly
vegetarians.

(5)
—

(10)
When the bear
cubs are 18
months old

(11)
—

(12)
the mother bear
leaves them
because they
can look after
themselves.

(13)
—

(18)
If there are too
many bears in an
open enclosure

(19)
—

(20)
they might not
like each other
and have a fight.

(21)
—

BACK COVER

© THURMAN 1983/84/85

If you would like to use this kind of storyboard to organize a fiction picture book, you might want to start by reading *Draw and Write Your Own Picture Book,* which Mark Thurman wrote with Emily Hearn (see page 40). Keep in mind that your illustrations will take up close to half of your book, so you will need to leave space for them, as the young authors did in the example.

There is no one way or "right way" to use a storyboard. If storyboards appeal to you, play around with them and figure out how they can help you. For example, I put my chapter headings, sub-headings, and boxes with the types of illustrations I want on my storyboard. I write the actual text for those pages on separate paper. I can refer back to my storyboard or erase it and change it as I go. It's sort of a visual table of contents!

The Plot Breakdown Repair Kit

Has your plot malfunctioned in the middle of your story? Try the Plot Breakdown Repair Kit!

Ask yourself the following questions. Answering them should help to resolve things and give you the details and reasons your characters need to be real and compelling.

1. Your Main Character(s)

- What are your main characters trying to achieve or become?

- Why are these achievements or changes so vital? What are your characters' reasons for wanting them?

- Have you set up incidents in your story so their reasons are clear?

2. The Person(s) or Thing(s) in the Way

- Are these obstacles clear in your mind?

- Why are these persons or things obstacles for your characters?

- Have you set up incidents or structured your dialogue so the obstacles and reasons are clear?

3. Setting Up the Initial Action and Complications

- What do your main characters do initially to achieve their goals?

- If this doesn't work, what do they do next?
- If this doesn't work, what do they do next?

4. The Crisis Point

- What is the decision your main characters make at the crucial point of having or not having their objective in their grasp?

5. Convincing the Reader

- Do the above four elements – characters, obstacles, action, crisis point – add up to an interesting story that will captivate your readers?

  If not, you need to go back and fine-tune it. Check which step doesn't seem to work. If it all seems to work well in your head, it's time to write it down.

"When I'm writing, it astonishes me
to find that things that happened at different points
in the book have come together in a satisfying unity
without my having planned it that way."

John Marsden, a popular Australian author for young adults

Creating Three-Dimensional Characters

Most stories begin when a circumstance we are caught in catches our imagination. We can see the main characters clearly, along with their dilemma and the possible solutions. In almost any type of fiction writing, you want your characters to be remembered by your reader. There has to be something about them that catches the reader's interest and emotions.

You also want your characters to have a sense of realism. Remember what it is like to hold a camera up to your eye, then place the subject of your photo within the small box of your camera lens? Beginning photographers are relieved if they manage not to cut off a friend's head during the shot, or they somehow avoid the ugly telephone pole in the background. Learning to write fully-developed characters takes imagination and practice.

"My characters get talked about at the dinner table as if they are real people."

Judy Blume, author of
ARE YOU THERE, GOD? IT'S ME, MARGARET

If you've managed to get the physical descriptions of your characters straight, you want to think next about what they are like as people. Can you hear their voices in your head? Is a particular character's voice high or deep? Quick or slow? What accents do they have? Being able to hear the voices may help you to write dialogue.

One way to make your characters more rounded is to know more about them than you need to know for the plot of your story. Imagine that you are meeting them for the first time, perhaps interviewing them on television. What would you want to ask them? What would you like to know about them?

Perhaps one of the best examples of character development is found in Christopher Finch's book, *Jim Henson: The Works: The Art, The Magic, The Imagination.* This book is a treasure-trove of psychological profiles of key Muppets including Big Bird, Kermit, Oscar the Grouch, and Grover. See how Bert and Ernie are described: "If Ernie is poetic, Bert is resolutely prosaic. He collects paper clips and is fascinated by the behavior of pigeons. Ernie has a carefree attitude toward the world; Bert is worried about everything. Not surprisingly, Bert and Ernie fight all the time, but they remain best friends."

___

"I was writing chapter three of HOMECOMING and out of the darkness of the typewriter, she leapt... I could hear what she was saying, and began making notes."

Cynthia Voigt, describing the creation of a character (Grandmother Tillerman) in her book, THE HOMECOMING

___

The Character Sheet

One of the most common mistakes young writers make is not developing their characters. Your characters may be your strength in your writing, or they may be your weakness. Let's see how your characters measure up!

Take two stories you have written. Select the one character in each story you have described best or are most fond of.

One trick to developing a fuller character is to anticipate and answer questions that might arise in the reader's mind about the character. The purpose of this exercise is to see what questions you normally answer when you sit down to write about a character.

On a new page in your Writer's Notebook, write these headings:

CHARACTER #1   CHARACTER #2

Now list these details for each character:

1. Name
2. Gender
3. Age
4. Height
5. Skin color
6. Hair color
7. Eye color
8. Clothes.

Now that you think about it, are there even more details you could add? You might start with these:

- non-physical details (likes, dislikes, hobbies)
- school
- favorite sayings
- something the character would be lost without
- how other family members perceive the character
- what makes the character sad, happy, mad.

Improving Characters and Dialogue

If your story has an adult character of your parents' or grandparents' age, and you are around your parents or grandparents often, try this for a day: Listen carefully to what they say. Do they have favorite words or expressions? Listen to what they say when you come home from school, when they are trying to encourage you, or when they are telling you to do something differently.

Notice how they stand when they speak. Notice how they sit when they relax. Do they have a favorite object they like to carry around with them? Do you know why, or have you ever asked them why? Record your observations, thoughts, and discoveries in your Writer's Notebook.

Now notice *yourself*. What do you say when you are annoyed, happy, confused? Look at yourself in the mirror and write a fully detailed description of what you see.

Have you noticed that people don't speak in the same way? They use different words and expressions. They also think totally different thoughts. Some people are joyous; others worry about particular things and then project their worries onto someone else. Make sure that your characters have their own specific dialogue.

In your Writer's Notebook, record the expressions and habits of people around you. This can be extremely helpful when you begin to develop a character.

Your main character may need space. Don't have too many characters fighting for center stage. Author Jean Little cut down the role of Jeremy's younger sister in *Mama's Going to Buy You a Mockingbird* because she was detracting from the story.

"I cannot shout loudly enough how important it is
to keep one's eyes open. If you long to write
or draw well – you must be willing to look, look and
look again with great concentration."

Maryanne Kovalski, children's author and illustrator

Gender Communication

In the early 1990s, books started appearing on the subject of "gender communication." Researchers like Deborah Tannen and others were finding that men and women not only communicated differently, they listened differently and resolved conflicts differently.

Here are examples of how a man and a woman might "hear" two statements:

- "I'll have to ask my wife/husband."
  The man hears: "This man is not in charge of his life."
  The woman hears: "This woman has an intimate relationship."

- "What's wrong?"
  The man hears: "This is a challenge."
  The woman hears: "This person wants more information."

There are many more, but this should be enough to give you a glimmer of what problems could occur, given that men and women have different ways of hearing and understanding the same statement.

In your Writer's Notebook, over a period of time (such as a school term), record disagreements that you hear and see people having. Ask yourself, "Are these people really trying to solve a problem, or is each person more committed to proving that he or she is right about something? Are they looking each other in the face and searching for clues as to how the other person is feeling? When they reconcile, is there any sign of forgiveness?" Also record any dialogue where it appears that two people have misunderstood each other.

Both of these exercises can be used for exploring characters and their dialogue in greater depth. If you'd like to learn more about gender communication, you can try reading chapters from this book:

- *You Just Don't Understand: Women and Men in Conversation* by Deborah Tannen (New York: Ballantine Books, 1994). It's written for adults but is also accessible for younger readers.

If you're interested in misunderstandings between teenagers and their parents, you might be interested in reading this book:

- *Bringing Up Parents: The Teenager's Handbook* by Alex J. Packer (Minneapolis: Free Spirit Publishing, 1992). It's written for teenagers, and it's so funny I laughed until I cried.

Mind Stretchers

Are you ready to exercise your imagination? In your Writer's Notebook, write a paragraph or so about each of these situations:

1. A space creature has arrived in your science classroom. She is only 2" high, but she can speak all Earth languages, and she is sitting right underneath your desk. Get underneath your desk and have a look at the classroom through her eyes. What does your teacher look like? Your books? The lights? Any of the unusual objects in your classroom? How do you look to her?

2. You wake up one morning to discover that you are a member of the opposite gender. Your bedroom clearly belongs to a member of the opposite gender. You shut your eyes, hoping that all will return to normal once you open them again. You open your eyes. Nothing has changed. You stifle a scream and run to the closet mirror. Describe what you look like. What are your thoughts? What clothes do you decide to put on? What is in your room? Now that you are a member of the opposite gender, what do you think of your parents? Your best friend? Your boyfriend/girlfriend?

Other short mind-stretchers to try:

- Do a character study of a person who doesn't seem to age, or who grows more beautiful/graceful/handsome as he/she gets older.

- Write a character study involving a teenager or adult who is learning the lesson that in order to get something he or she wants, he or she has to give something first. For example, a young woman wants more love but hasn't realized that she has to be more loving. Or a young man wants more respect but hasn't yet figured out that he has to be more respectful.

If you are interested in more of these types of activities, you might try my book for teachers:

- *The Writing Coach: Strategies for Helping Students Develop Their Own Writing Voice* by Janet E. Grant (Markham: Pembroke, 1992). In the United States, contact The Wright Group, 1-800-523-2371.

Creating Settings that Come Alive

Do your settings sound as if the same interior designer has decorated all of your characters' houses and rooms? Curious about whether a film set decorator could offer any specific advice to young writers about the importance of settings, I spoke with Jenny Dyer, who worked on *The Saint-Exupéry Story,* a biography of the famous French author of *The Little Prince.* She shared with me some of the things she has to think about when decorating a set.

● ● ● ● ●

Thoughts of a Set Decorator
by Jenny Dyer

IT IS ESSENTIAL to create an environment that is right for your character. You should use lots of sources to work from – photographs, classical paintings, and visits, if possible, to art galleries. For example, I've seen one room set that was based on a particular Impressionist painting, because the essence of the painting brought out an emotion that was being communicated in the film.

Here are some other things you will want to be sure to keep in mind:

1. **Color.** Color manipulates emotions. Just think how a room painted black can make you feel uncomfortable, while a room painted white creates a feeling of lightness and air. A darker color will suggest a gloomy, oppressed atmosphere; a lighter color suggests free-spiritedness. In *The Saint-Exupéry Story,* because roses are a prevalent theme in *The Little Prince,* one room was painted to look a dark color, but on closer examination, the pattern was visible as hundreds of roses.

2. **Fabric and Texture.** Remind yourself of how certain fabrics and textures feel against your skin. For example, think of velvet, which is soft and sensuous; then think of burlap, which is abrasive and uncomfortable. People who live in luxury might have velvet drapes; people who live in poverty might have burlap drapes or paper shades.

3. **Small Belongings.** Every handbag, every pen, every little item tells a story in itself. It must be suitable and reinforce the character. For example, someone quite affluent might have possessions of silver or marble; someone without money might have possessions of wood or cheap metal. In *The Saint-Exupéry Story,* they used electric lights, which in turn-of-the-century France was a luxury available to wealthy families.

4. **Plants and Gardens.** You might show the progress of time or a change in someone's life in the plants and/or gardens they keep. The garden was a very big issue in *The Saint-Exupéry Story.* The children had a secret garden where they went to play. It was the only place they felt was their own. It was designed with white flowers to communicate childhood innocence. Years later, when Saint-Exupéry revisited the garden, he found it overgrown. This time, the garden had red flowers, symbolizing that the main character had entered a time in his life where there was passion (he had fallen in love) and color.

● ● ● ● ●

In your own settings, you might want to consider color, lighting, small belongings (if you haven't already done so in your character sketch), plants, gardens, and vegetation. Also, when you are writing settings, close your eyes and pretend that *you are the character,* actually seeing that particular setting at that particular time of day in that particular weather. Better yet, if you can, visit the place you are describing or a similar place to get a sense of the smells, colors, atmosphere, and so on. Take notes and bring them home with you.

Watch for certain places you visit that seem to get your artistic juices rolling or give a particular type of "hum." I experience this when I walk into the Egyptian room at the British Museum, when I walk around the Jersey Zoo, when I am in airports, and when I am around particularly old wonderfully designed buildings. There are probably places where you experience this, too. Where are those places?

When you go to a library or a bookstore, look for books shelved under "Interiors" or "Interior Decorating." Books and exhibition catalogs published by museums and art galleries about different historical periods also make excellent references.

READING CHALLENGE

▸ *Against Nature* by J.K. Huysmans (London: Penguin Classics, 1959). A fascinating book by a man who turned away from society and built a rather unusual but special house.

Improving Settings

Take a story you have written. Take a setting from it. Then think of a place resembling that setting that you live close to or have a photo of. Go to the place or take out the photo. Look at it closely. Can you see anything you may have missed in your description? Have you caught the colors, the textures, the smells? Jot down details and discoveries in your Writer's Notebook.

Re-read what you have written about that setting, then improve your setting with the added description and details you have picked up from your study.

Rewriting

The willingness to rewrite and create the best piece possible is a sign of a conscientious writer. Oftentimes, young writers have one part of their story or article down pat. When I give feedback, I usually try to help the young writer focus on one element of their writing that needs work. Some examples:

• "Kara, you seem to have a really good grip on your dialogue. How about digging into your settings more so we can see where your characters live? How long do you think that will take you? By next week? Fine. Will you show it to me then?"

- "John, your images are much stronger. Congratulations. What do you think about the plot structure? You lost me at this point in your story. What were you trying to say or have happen? Oh, really? Good. Can you rewrite that and let me see it tomorrow?"

- "Trudi, do you want to make this short story into a novel? We'll just be working on short stories this term, but if you would like to explore ways of making it into a novel, why not read Lee Wyndham's *Writing for Children and Teenagers* for some tips?"

"I was working on the proof of one of my poems all morning, and took out a comma. In the afternoon, I put it back again."

Attributed to playwright Oscar Wilde

Rate Your Writing

Look closely at something you have written – a short story, children's book, fantasy story, play, or anything else you think is a good example of your writing. Then rate each of the following elements. Give yourself a 3 for "Excellent," a 2 for "Fair," and a 1 for "Needs Work." Record your ratings in your Writer's Notebook.

- Characters
- Use of language
- Plot
- Setting
- Knowledge of genre.

Then answer these questions:

- What do you like best about your writing?
- What do you like least about it?
- What would you like to improve?
- What can you do to improve?

Reading Your Work Aloud

A great way to get feedback on your writing is by reading your work aloud to others. Some people are masters at reading their own work, and others are barely able to get the words out. There is probably nothing more disappointing for a group of avid readers than to go to a reading and find that the author doesn't read very well. (If you have ever attended authors' readings, you probably know what I am talking about. No wonder so many audio versions of books are read by professional actors!)

Here are five tips that will help you to be a better reader:

1. Stand up straight and speak clearly.
2. Make sure the whole room can hear you. (Ask, "Can everyone hear me? All the way in the back?")
3. Pronounce individual words clearly.
4. Take a breath once in a while to make sure you aren't speeding through your work.
5. Change the tone and pitch of your voice for different characters.

If you really want to improve your read-aloud skills, try one or more of these:

- Join a storytelling group to learn techniques in storytelling.

- Listen to tapes of well-recorded books. Books on tape are very popular today, especially useful for long trips in the car or by bus. Some of them are abridged; some are full-length; some are read by the authors; and some are read by professional actors and actresses. Most bookstores and libraries carry a selection, and some video stores have them available for rent.

- Listen to radio broadcasts of author readings, check network and cable TV channels for programs featuring authors reading their books, or attend author readings at schools, libraries, bookstores, or art centers. Various radio stations in the United States carry programs on writers reading their work. Tune in to the arts program of a local radio station, or call the nearest public radio station for information. In England, Radio 4's "Book at Bedtime" is the easiest way to hear books read aloud. (They aren't always read by the authors, however.) In Toronto, Canada, there are readings all year round at Harbourfront, an arts complex that I consider one of the most beautiful places in the world. Internationally renowned authors come to Harbourfront to read from their recent works.

- Most importantly, always take the opportunity to read your work aloud – in your writers' support group, or with a friend at home or school. Ask someone you respect to rate your reading aloud on a scale of 1–10. Get constructive comments about how you can improve.

"When I read I try to sound like I'm not reading,
like I'm instead the old uncle on the back porch
bullslinging away."

Lesley Choyce, author of An Avalanche of Ocean

● ● ● ● ●

Thoughts on My Writing

by Peter Saunders, 16

I LOVE TO DESCRIBE. This shows in my writing. I love to imagine things and then tell the world about them, on paper. I love to create, both through words and through pictures, although I am much better with words than with pictures, for with words, I can describe things which I could never draw. Although not all of my best work is fiction, my favorite is.

I do not love to write dialogue. I am always attempting to make good use of this particular element of writing, but my words begin to sound unnatural when they are meant to be spoken. Thus, I am more likely to describe a scene through adjectives than through the speech of the characters.

I do not pretend to know a lot about writing. At this stage, I am an amateur; nothing more. I do not write enough, but I strive to be published with some regularity. My writing is still quite juvenile; I often rewrite stories I wrote years before, making extensive changes, and sometimes inventing an entirely new plot.

My writing is getting better. In fact, the improvements are obvious. They are what keep me going. My most recent story is almost always my favorite story in the world.... I love my writing. If I didn't, I wouldn't do it at all.

● ● ● ● ●

RECOMMENDED READING

Here is a select list of books that can help you with all aspects of
your writing.

- *Becoming a Writer* by Dorothea Brande (Los Angeles: Jeremy P.
  Tarcher, 1981). Practical ideas on how to increase the amount of
  words you write in one sitting, plus how to overcome any "writer's
  block."

- *Can You Find It? 25 Library Scavenger Hunts to Sharpen Your
  Research Skills* by Randall McCutcheon (Minneapolis: Free Spirit
  Publishing, 1991). Without a doubt the funniest book I've encoun-
  tered on finding anything. A definite must for young writers
  looking for unusual research material.

- *Characters and Viewpoint* by Orson Scott Card (Cincinnati, OH:
  Writer's Digest Books, 1988). You may be familiar with some of
  Orson Scott Card's wonderful characters through his short stories
  and science fiction novels, including *Ender's Game* and *Seventh Son.*

- *Creating Characters: How to Build Story People* by Dwight V. Swain
  (Cincinnati, OH: Writer's Digest Books, 1994).

- *Dialogue* by Lewis Turco (Cincinnati, OH: Writer's Digest Books,
  1989).

- *How to Write a Mi££ion* by Ansen Dibell, Orson Scott Card, and
  Lewis Turco (London: Robinson Publishing, 1994). This is the
  United Kingdom compilation of *Plot* by Ansen Dibell, *Characters
  and Viewpoint* by Orson Scott Card, and *Dialogue* by Lewis Turco,
  published in the United States as individual volumes.

- *Make Your Own Book: A Complete Kit* (Philadelphia: Running
  Press, 1993). This activity kit is a fun way to learn the art of making books. It's particularly useful if you want to make a special
  present of your writing. Includes *The Bookmaking Handbook* by
  Matthew Liddle.

- *Nonfiction for Children: How to Write It, How to Sell It* by Ellen
  E.M. Roberts (Cincinnati, OH: Writer's Digest Books, 1986). Takes
  you step-by-step through the different requirements of each children's age group.

▶ *Plot* by Ansen Dibell (Cincinnati, OH: Writer's Digest Books, 1988). This is one of the most constructive discussions of plot I have seen. I would happily place this book in the hands of any young writer who is interested in writing longer fiction.

▶ *The Power of Your Other Hand: A Course in Channeling the Inner Wisdom of the Right Brain* by Lucia Capachione (Van Nuys, CA: Newcastle Publishing Co., 1988). Write with your "other hand" (not the one you usually write with) and discover a different side of your writing! A fascinating book.

▶ *Use Your Head* by Tony Buzan (London: BBC Publications, 1993). My all-time favorite book on understanding the brain, plus how to study more effectively, read quicker, research sensibly, and develop your own ways of thinking. The United States edition is *Use Both Sides of Your Brain* (New York: NAL-Dutton, 1991).

▶ *Writing for Children and Teenagers,* 3rd edition, by Lee Wyndham and Arnold Madison (Cincinnati, OH: Writer's Digest Books, 1988). Suggests the synopsis approach. Highly recommended for writers who get stuck in the middle of their stories or want to know how to move from a short story to a novel.

CHAPTER FIVE

Finding the Right Publishers

THE PUBLISHING INDUSTRY is a complex one. If you could imagine a gigantic Monopoly board (for the United States industry alone), with thousands of book and magazine publishers, thousands of independent bookstores, a handful of major bookstore chains, thousands of writers, etc. etc., you can start to see what I mean by complex. But the process of finding the right place to get published is a relatively simple one that you can get better at with time and experience.

There are literally tens of thousands of publishers around the world. The publishing industry (primarily because it deals with information and trends) constantly changes. One year, a particular type of book is all the rage; three years later, no one seems to be buying those books anymore. (For example, books about the environment were hot in the early 1990s; they are much less so now.) One year, your publishing company may be bought by another company; five years later, it may be bought by yet another company.

The point of this chapter is to reduce the amount of unnecessary work you might do in finding the most suitable publishers for your writing. The reason I say "publishers" (plural) rather than "publisher" (singular) is because, depending on your writing, there may be more than one publisher interested in it.

Most professional authors find out where to get published by:

- asking other authors
- referring to market guides

- asking editors they might know, or
- sending their manuscripts to an agent.

  Most young writers find out where to get published by:
- referring to market guides (especially the *Market Guide for Young Writers*; see page 90)
- going to bookstores and libraries and checking out publishers who specialize in their type of writing
- asking teachers, relatives, or friends of their parents for advice
- finding out about writing contests
- making inquiries at their local newspaper or the office of a favorite magazine, or
- asking professional authors.

The Right Fit

Have you ever gone shopping for jeans and been in such a rush that you grabbed the first pair that seemed to fit? Then, when you got home, you found that they fit okay but not perfectly? That's similar to what happens to many novice writers who are trying to get published. They are in such a rush that they send their manuscript off to the first publisher they *think* is right. They wait hopefully. Then they eventually receive a rejection slip because the publisher doesn't publish that type of writing.

Simon French, an Australian author for young adults, tells this story about trying to get his first novel published: "I looked through the Yellow Pages and started sending it [his manuscript] off. It was returned five times, partly because I sent it to people who did not publish children's books.... Later someone told me that A&R [a publisher] had a new editor, so I mailed it off to them again."

One way to think about publishers is to think of two stores you often go to that sell the same type of merchandise (clothing, CDs, jewelry, or whatever). Who are the designers, the manufacturers, the makers, the labels whose products you buy? Why do you sometimes buy from one type of clothing designer, and at other times buy from another? What is it that you expect from them?

A publisher is really no different from a clothing designer, record label, jewelry designer, or whatever. Each publisher tries to develop a particular look or "list" of books. The publisher will have spent years developing a particular line of books or a particular look to a magazine.

You can't expect to sell your science fiction book to a publisher that specializes in romance. But you would be surprised by how many novice writers send their writing to the wrong publishers. They keep doing this until the day they realize that they are wasting their time. With a few hours of research, you can find the right fit for your writing.

"Literature is like any other trade; you will never sell anything unless you go to the right shop."
Playwright George Bernard Shaw

As you read this chapter, please keep this very important point in mind: Submitting your writing for publication, whether to a magazine or a national contest, is a very personal decision. All writers have their own reasons for submitting their work for publication. The reasons can range from wanting to earn money to wanting to influence people's ideas and attitudes. *There is no need to feel that you have to get published, or even that you have to try to get published, right now.* If you aren't ready yet, wait until you are.

When you do feel ready, you'll want to know that there are three types of publishers you can approach with your writing:

- young writers' publishers (you'll find out more about them in the next section),

- educational publishers (they publish the novels and textbooks you use in school, and the books your teachers and professors use), and

- mainstream publishers (also called "trade publishers," they produce most of the books you find in bookstores).

Exciting Times

There are exciting publishing opportunities for young writers today, especially in North America and particularly in the young writers' publishers market. This market has developed in recent years to include over 150 places specifically designed to encourage and publish young writers. They are staffed by people who think it is important for young writers' work to gain an audience. This market consists primarily of contests run by mainstream publishers, and magazines that publish young writers' work and also run contests.

For example, each year three young writers ages 6–19 win a $5,000 scholarship and receive royalties for their first book as winners of a North American contest. Another 14 writers ages 7–14 win $500 in a Canadian contest. And each month, dozens of young writers are published in magazines in Canada and the United States.

The *best* source of information about these publishers and contests is:

- *Market Guide for Young Writers,* 4th edition, by Kathy Henderson (Cincinnati, OH: Writer's Digest Books, 1993).

Although some young writers are published by mainstream publishers, their numbers are very small. When young writers send their work to these publishers, they are up against professional writers, sometimes including their own favorite authors! Of the few who do get published, most have already won awards, or they have had a teacher, another author, or an editor they know read their work and recognize it as exceptional. To prove that it is possible (although difficult) for young writers to publish their work with mainstream publishers, here are ten success stories.

1. **Jessica Caroll.** Jessica wrote *Billy the Punk,* a book for children ages 6 and up, when she was 12. It was published by Random House in Australia when she was 17.

2. **Zlata Filipovic.** In 1992, Zlata, age 11, wrote a diary by candlelight, recording the war in Sarajevo, the city she lived in. Her teacher

told her about UNICEF's plan to publish a child's diary about the war, and soon *Zlata's Diary* was published and translated into 23 languages. With the help of the French government, Zlata and her parents fled from Sarajevo to Paris.

3. **Simon French.** Born in 1957 in Sydney, Australia, Simon French was co-editor of a short-lived school newspaper during his high school years. He wrote his first novel, *Hey Phanton Singlet,* when he was 15. It was published three years later, in 1975, by Angus and Robertson.

4. **S.E. Hinton.** Concerned with the way people were stereotyping gangs of young people, Susan Hinton, while still attending high school, wrote a 40-page story that grew into the best-selling *The Outsiders.* It was published by Dell in New York in 1967.

5. **Wendy Isdell.** In 1992, high school student Wendy Isdell sent a story to a publisher along with a letter beginning, "I have a proposition which may interest you. In the fall of 1988 I started writing a book...." Her story had already won first place in the Virginia Young Authors' Contest of 1989. Wendy's book, *A Gebra Named Al,* was published by Free Spirit Publishing in 1993, when Wendy was a senior. (Wendy also wrote a teacher's guide to accompany her book.)

6. **Gordon Korman.** Gordon Korman wrote *This Can't Be Happening at MacDonald Hall* as the result of a seventh-grade school assignment. Published in 1977 by Scholastic in Toronto, it was the first in a series of young adult novels by Korman.

7. **Nicole Luiken.** Nicole Luiken started to write during her hour-long bus ride to school in Alberta, Canada. In 1988, when she was 17, her manuscript, *Unlocking the Doors,* was published by Scholastic in Toronto.

8. **Caitlin Moran.** At the age of 15, Caitlin used her experience as a home-schooled child in a large family in England as the basis for her first novel, *Chronicles of Narmo.* It was published simultaneously in Great Britain by Corgi Books and by Doubleday in London in 1992.

9. **Christopher Nolan.** In Ireland, school-aged Christopher Nolan, unable to use his limbs or to speak, used a "unicorn stick" fastened to his forehead to hit the keys of a typewriter. He won a special prize in a British society's literary competition – twice! His first book of poetry, *Dam-burst of Dreams,* was accepted when he was 14, published in 1981 (by Weidenfeld and Nicolson in London), and published again in 1988 by Ohio University Press.

"I had a telephone call from Weidenfeld's. 'Yes, we're interested,' they said. In fact, they told me to tell you that they feel privileged to have been allowed to read your work and they would be honored to publish it."

Christopher Nolan's mother, telling Christopher about her conversation with a publisher; reported in his autobiography, Under the Eye of the Clock

---

10. **David Binney Putnam.** In the 1920s, when he was a teenager, David Binney Putnam traveled with his famous publisher father, George Putnam, to the Galapagos Islands. On his return home, he wrote *David Goes Voyaging.* Published in 1925 by G.P. Putnam's Sons in New York, it became the first in a series of books for boys.

Remember that these are the exceptions! Although it appears that more and more young people are getting published by mainstream publishers, especially during the past five years or so, the reality is that it is still very difficult to "break in." If you compare the numbers, you'll see why I advise almost all young writers to start off in the young writers' publishers market.

Market Guides

The best place to learn about publishers is in the reference books, called "market guides," that all professional writers use. Most countries have a *Writer's Market* or *Writer's Handbook* listing book and magazine publishers. These books can be 1½" to 2" thick. Don't be put off by their size. Once you learn how to use one, you will refer to it often.

The best advice I can give you is to get a copy of Kathy Henderson's *Market Guide for Young Writers,* which is specifically designed to introduce the young writer to a market guide. Then move on to market guides written for adults. Some of these are *The Writer's Market, Poet's Market,* and *Short Story and Novel Market.* Choose the one or ones that seem best suited to your interests and needs.

To get the most out of a market guide written for adults, start by looking at the table of contents. Check off the sections that are of interest to you (or list them on a separate piece of paper, if you're using someone else's copy or a library copy). At first, try to read just a few entries. During your next time through, work out a system of highlighting or underlining the publishers that interest you.

Writer's Market, published by Writer's Digest in the United States (the resource book for both Canadian and American writers), has a section called "Using Writer's Market," which gives you some help. *The Writer's Handbook,* published in England by Macmillan/PEN, has a table of contents from which you can work your way through the book. You can also go to the library and read *The Literary Market Place* and such magazines as *Publishers Weekly, Writer's Digest, The Writer,* and *ByLine.*

Again, the most realistic place for a young writer to start is where most young writers are getting published. Years of experience have shown that the best route is to go through Kathy Henderson's *Market Guide for Young Writers,* or the Contest listings in your country's *Writer's Market* or *Writer's Handbook,* and find the competitions and/or magazines that are most appealing to you.

Checking Out Libraries and Bookstores

Another way to find publishers is to check out your library at home, your local library or school media center, or local bookstores. Bring your Writer's Notebook along to take notes.

Look for books that are written in the genre you prefer to work in. Find out who the publishers are. Write down this information in your Writer's Notebook.

You will always find the publisher's name on the copyright page of a book. That is the page where you will also find the author's name, the year the book was published, and the ISBN number, which is very helpful if you want to order a copy of the book for yourself. (Check the copyright page for this book if you want to see an example.)

Contests and Awards

Following is a very brief listing of contests and awards specifically for young writers. Write to the addresses shown if you would like to know how to enter or qualify. For more complete listings for the United States and Canada, see the *Market Guide for Young Writers.*

Australia

The Kitty Archer-Burton Award
Awarded biennially (every two years) for verse by a young writer under age 19. For information, write to: Federal President, Society of Women Writers (Australia), GPO Box 1388, Sydney, NSW 2001, Australia.

National Book Council/Angus and Robertson Fiction Prize
Entrants must be Australian residents and at least 18 years of age. Pays a $10,000 advance on royalties. For information, write to: Executive

Secretary, NBC, Suite 3, 21 Drummond Place, Carlton, Victoria 3035, Australia.

Canada

Air Canada Award
Awarded by the Canadian Authors Association to a Canadian writer under age 30 deemed to show the most promise in the field of literary creation. For information, write to: C.A.A., 275 Slater St., Suite 500, Ottawa, Ontario, K1P 5H9, Canada.

The Prism Award
A national short-story contest for young writers ages 7–14. Two age categories: 7–10 and 11–14. For information, write to: The Prism Awards, 90 Venice Crescent, Thornhill, Ontario, L4J 7T1, Canada.

YTV Achievement Award
Awarded to a promising young writer under age 19. For information, write to: YTV Canada, Inc., YTV Achievement Awards, P.O. Box 1060, Station B, Toronto, Ontario, M5T 2T8, Canada.

United Kingdom

Authors' Club Best First Novel Award
Award for the most promising first novel of the year. Entries for the award are accepted from publishers. For information, write to: The Authors' Club, 40 Dover Street, London W1X 3RB, England.

BBC Wildlife Awards for Nature Writing
Prize for the best essay on nature by a young writer age 17 and under. Also a prize for the 12 and under age group. For information, write to: BBC Wildlife Magazine, Broadcasting House, Whiteladies Road, Bristol BS8 2LR, England.

E.C. Gregory Trust Fund Awards
Submission of a published or unpublished volume of poetry, drama poems, or *belles-lettres* (light, stylish writing on literary or intellectual subjects). Open to writers under age 30. For information, write to: Society of Authors, 84 Drayton Gardens, London SW10 9SB, England.

Unicorn Theater Young Playwright's Competition

For young playwrights in three age groups: 4–6, 7–9, and 10–12. The play is performed after a workshop with a member of the Theater Club. For information, write to: Unicorn Theater for Children, Arts Theater, Great Newport Street, London WC2H 7JB, England.

United States

Delacorte First Young Adult Novel Contest

Annual contest for American and Canadian writers for a book-length manuscript with a contemporary setting. For information, write to: Delacorte Press, Department BFYR, 666 Fifth Avenue, New York, NY 10103, U.S.A.

NWA Novel Contest

Annual contest for novel manuscript in any genre. For information, write to: National Writers Association, 1450 S. Havana, Suite 620, Aurora, CO 80012, U.S.A.

National Written & Illustrated By...Awards Contest for Students

Three age categories: 6–9, 10–13, and 14–19. Each entry must be written and illustrated by the same student. For complete rules and guidelines, send a self-addressed, stamped, business-size envelope with 58 cents in postage to: Landmark Editions, Inc., 1402 Kansas Avenue, Kansas City, MO 64127, U.S.A.

Should You Enter a National Contest?

Usually school experiences leave us with a sense that we should start off submitting things locally. Then, and only then, if we are any good, should we move up to compete in our state, province, or country. Sending our manuscripts out of the country may feel very unnatural.

Rarely do I find that young writers have a market waiting for them in their own home town or city. There might be a few local publications or contests, but they may not be the right ones for their work. The market for your work may indeed be in your state, province, country...or even another country. Don't be put off by the fact that a contest you enter is hundreds or thousands of miles away. It may be the perfect place for you to enter. It can also be rather exciting – and a real learning experience besides, as Kristin Pedersen discovered.

• • • • •

Thoughts from a Contest Winner
by Kristin Pedersen, 19

BEING CHOSEN AS A WINNER in Landmark Editions' National Written & Illustrated By…Awards Contest for Students taught me a lot about what a publisher is looking for. In order to support their company, they need to find an audience to buy your book, and so they look for a book that the audience will like. Here is a brief summary of some audience-pleasing techniques I learned while editing my book at Landmark's office:

- What's unique about your book? Is it the way you've illustrated it? Is it your story idea? Having an original, creative slant to a book increases its appeal.

- When you write a picture book, you will most likely be writing for two audiences – the child who will want the book, and the adult who will buy it. A successful picture book will be one that both audiences find appealing.

- It's a good idea to decide on definite ages for the characters. Why? Picture books are aimed towards certain age groups of kids who will want to identify with your characters. For instance, an eight-year-old will probably want to read about a ten-year-old or even an older adult driving a real truck, rather than reading about a two-year-old playing with a toy truck.

- Picture books usually need to be rewritten, just as novels do. Take a good look at your story, and decide what needs to be revised. Then read it to family, friends, or other people and see if they have any constructive suggestions. Children and adults are all around you. If you read your work to them, you will likely get suggestions as well as praise! My experience has been that others are eager to see what you write.

When I visited Landmark's offices, the editors spent a lot of time with me as I worked on my story and illustrations. I learned a lot about how professional and concise a published work needs to be. It was a terrific experience!

● ● ● ● ●

The Author/Editor/Publisher Link

Most of the books and magazines we read today are designed, printed, and distributed by someone other than the author. The author is responsible for producing the finest writing possible, turning the manuscript in on time, and working with the editor to make any changes needed to produce a final, publishable manuscript.

The author works closely with the editor. An editor is someone who is hired by the publisher to prepare books and articles for publication. This includes making corrections, asking the author to make any needed revisions, and working with the production and design department to turn the author's manuscript into a finished book or article. Most editors have a certain page length or word count in mind.

The publisher is responsible for producing and distributing the books, magazines, and related materials. The publisher is also responsible for keeping the business operating, which means turning a profit. The publishing industry is a business. Just as your local grocery store can't stay in business if it doesn't sell enough groceries, publishing houses can't stay in business if they can't sell enough books or magazines. The materials they publish need to sell. Most publishers have a good idea of what they can sell. They look for certain types of writing on certain topics.

How can you establish a good author/editor/publisher link? Submit your work to a publisher only after you've really looked at the market. Submitting your manuscript and waiting for a reply can take a long time, so you want to make sure to send it to the most suitable publishers from the start. Don't waste your time and effort sending it to the wrong places. Do your research first! The industry may not make a lot of sense to you right now, but slowly the pieces of the puzzle will start to fall into place.

A Special Note for Nonfiction Writers

A young unpublished nonfiction writer is researching possible publishers for his book with a very unusual angle on Lewis Carroll, author of *Alice in Wonderland*. He finds three publishers that already have books on Lewis Carroll. He thinks to himself, "I shouldn't send my book to them, because it will just be competing with what they have. I'll find a publisher that doesn't have *any* books on my topic."

He has just made a very common mistake. In fact, the publishers with books on Lewis Carroll are the *first* places he should send his book to for consideration. In the same way, you are more likely to get your book accepted by a publisher that already has one or more successful books in your subject area.

Spend some time flipping through *current* nonfiction books at your bookstore or library. For each, stop and read the author's "Acknowledgments" page. This will sometimes give you an idea of what the editor was like to work with. Try to get a broad, general sense of the topics and angles each publisher seems interested in publishing. Then make your own judgments about which publishers seem right for you.

Finding the Right Publishers

The purpose of this exercise is to teach you the steps all writers have to go through if they would like to have a piece of writing published. With time, you will build up a working knowledge of which publishers are most likely to be right for you. But in the beginning, you need to take these basic steps.

Don't shy away from this exercise. It will teach you all sorts of interesting things. You'll see your first publisher's catalog. You may even find new books of interest to you. (I found a superb book by Peter Dickinson, *Eva*, because it was listed as winning a number of awards on the back pages of the Delacorte Press catalog.)

Take one of your own written pieces to make this exercise work, preferably one you would like to get published eventually, or one that is written in the same genre you would like to get published in someday. If it doesn't yet have a title, give it a working (temporary) title.

The sample Writer's Notebook page shown on page 101 illustrates the steps you need to take in determining what publishers you would like to submit your work to. The directions that follow here explain each step in the process. Write down the things you do for each step in your own Writer's Notebook. You may want to start a separate page for each genre or area you are interested in.

Step 1: Determine your favorite genre – the one you would like to be published in. (Remember that genres are the subject of Chapter Three. You may want to re-read that chapter before doing this step.)

Step 2: Write down several names of publishers (of books and/or magazines) that publish writing in the genre you have chosen. If you can't name any, go to some books or magazines in that genre and find the publisher's name. For books, you'll find it on the copyright page or the spine of the book. For magazines, you'll find it on the masthead (usually somewhere on the first few pages, along with the names of editors, contributors, etc.). If you are able to think of only one publisher's name, you definitely need to become familiar with market guides.

Step 3: Write down the title (or working title) of the piece of writing you are using for this exercise.

Step 4: Write down the names of the publishers you would like to have this piece published by. Try to name at least three.

Now go back to Step 2 and double-check your list to make sure you haven't missed a potential market.

Step 5: Find the name of the editor who is responsible for your genre at each of the three publishers you have listed. You can usually find the editor's name in the publisher's listing in the *Writer's Market* or *Market Guide.*

Step 6: Write to the publishers you have selected and request their most recent catalogs. If you are approaching a magazine publisher, ask for their guidelines. If you can't get a copy of the magazine, they will usually send you a copy for a small fee plus postage.

FINDING THE RIGHT PUBLISHER

Step 1: Favorite Genre:

Young Adult Novel

Step 2: Publishers:

Penguin, Avon, Scholastic

Step 3: Title of My Work:

<u>Blue</u>

Step 4: Publishers to Contact:

Avon, Delacorte, Scholastic

Step 5: Editors' Names

Avon: check current <u>Writer's Market</u>

Delacorte: check current <u>Writer's Market</u>

Scholastic: check current <u>Writer's Market</u>

Step 6: Catalogs

Sent for: Yes (all 3) November 15.

Received:

Avon – yes

Delacorte – not yet

Scholastic – yes

Now you need to sort through all the information you have gathered.

- **For a book publisher,** study the catalog carefully. This will tell you a lot about the publisher's emphasis and direction. Does the type of books it publishes seem like a good fit for your work? If so, great. You have found a publisher you can keep an eye on for years to come. If the catalog doesn't seem to fit what you had in mind, cross that name off your list and select another publisher to check out. Some publishers have many catalogs (adult, children, business, education, psychology, etc.). Make sure to get the one that is right for you.

- **For a magazine publisher,** study the magazine and guidelines carefully. Does it really publish the type of articles you see yourself writing? If not, cross it off your list and find another.

What this exercise does is let you fine-tune your thinking about your writing and where you see it being published. For example, you may have had high hopes of publishing your short story with a particular teen magazine, only to find on reading last year's contest winners that the magazine doesn't accept historical fiction.

The Tip of the Iceberg

Finding suitable publishers takes time, yet it also builds important skills. Along the way, you'll learn more about the audience you are writing for, set a date for finishing your piece, finish it on time, prepare it for submission (described in Chapter Six), and decide where to send it.

You may write a nonfiction article about a hobby and have no qualms about submitting it to a publisher. On the other hand, you may write a short story, then hesitate to send it off because you're worried about whether it's good enough. While these concerns are only natural, it is useful to keep this question in mind: "What do I *really* want?" Focus on that instead of your self-doubts.

Trying to get your writing published is a positive experience either way. If you *don't* get published, you are learning that:

- your writing is not appropriate for the publisher you selected (very important to know), or

- you need to work on your writing some more, or

- perhaps other, more uncontrollable factors are involved:
  - the publisher's editor turned down your piece because the book probably wouldn't sell enough copies to make money
  - the publisher already has a book like yours signed for the coming season
  - the editor doesn't like it personally

- the publisher doesn't like it, or
- like Madeleine L'Engle, author of *A Wrinkle in Time,* you are 10 years ahead of the publishing market. (Yes, it took 10 years and many rejections before her award-winning classic was accepted for publication.)

If you *do* get published, you are developing confidence in being able to write for a particular market, magazine, or contest. You're gaining a readership. You're finding places to air your opinions, thoughts, and views, and to showcase your talents as a writer.

Having a book or article accepted for publication is like reaching the tip of an iceberg. You have probably spent a lot of time trying to get there, and when you do, you discover that there are many things happening below the water line. All sorts of questions about how the publishing industry works will bob up to the surface. How do books get promoted? How does a person become a famous writer? The answers to these questions come with experience – and with reading more books, talking to more authors and publishers, and submitting more works for publication. Give it time. You're just beginning!

As a young writer, you can bring your own authentic voice to not only books, but also brochures, videos, radio shows – anything, in fact, aimed at teenagers or about teenagers. For example, Lana Israel wrote a teen version of Tony Buzan's *Use Your Head* while still in school. And there are many more excellent adult nonfiction books that desperately need a teen version (such as Richard Bolles's *What Color Is Your Parachute?*, to name just one). Plus, on a lighter note, I think the greeting-card market is ripe for some teen input.

● ● ● ● ●

Breaking into Publishing
by Jennifer Carnell, 18

I WROTE MY FIRST NOVEL, a children's book called *The Return of Count Dracula,* when I was 13 years old. It was submitted to an agent and to numerous British publishers, but unfortunately it received an equal number of rejections. In retrospect, I can see that this was not so very surprising, because while I still think that the book was extremely good for my age, it was not a particularly original story, and there was too much plot crammed into 180 pages, making it seem overdone. Sadly, rejection slips seem to be almost inevitable when one is trying to be published, and although it can be very depressing you should not give up, nor assume that just because one publisher turns you down that another will do the same.

Three years later, I had better luck when I wrote an adult novel, entitled *Murder, Mystery and Mayhem,* which is a comic pastiche of the English detective novels of the nineteen thirties, which I hoped would appeal to publishers more than the earlier novel's theme of dastardly doings of vampires. To my delight, Collins publishers expressed an interest in the work. They asked me to do some rewriting (to lengthen a rushed ending), after which it was accepted and published by Collins in Great Britain and Australia, and a year later in the United States by HarperCollins.

The time of publication was very exciting, particularly seeing the front cover, and I was asked to do newspaper, radio, and television interviews, which was both interesting and nerve-wracking. This led on to other things, as I was asked to write several articles and review books and I was also eligible to join the Crime Writers Association, which gives me the opportunity to meet other writers.

If you do succeed in getting published, be sure to seek out advice from other people, as publishers run a business and may not always tell you things unless you ask! Lastly, good luck!

● ● ● ● ●

"For several days after my first book was published
I carried it about in my pocket,
and took surreptitious peeps at it to make sure
the ink had not faded."

Sir James M. Barrie, author of PETER PAN

RECOMMENDED READING

▸ *Children's Writer's & Illustrator's Market,* edited by Christine Martin (Cincinnati, OH: Writer's Digest Books, updated annually).

▸ *Dear Writer: Advice to Aspiring Writers* by C. Bird (London: Virago, 1990).

▸ *How to Get Happily Published,* 4th edition, by Judith Appelbaum and Nancy Evans (New York: Harper Reference Books, 1992).

▸ *How to Write a Book and Get It Published: A Complete Guide to the Publishing Maze* by S. Curran (London: Thorsons, 1990).

▸ *Thirty Ways to Make Money in Writing* by J. Hawthorne (London: Rosters, 1989).

▸ *The Writer's Handbook* (London: Macmillan/PEN, updated annually). This is primarily a sourcebook of publishers, literary associations, newspapers, and local radio, film, television, and video producers, etc. for the United Kingdom. United States book publishers and agents are listed in separate sections. For young writers, there are important sections in addition to the market listings: "Arts Councils and Regional Arts Boards," "Courses, Circles, and Workshops," and "Prizes."

▸ *Writers & Artists Yearbook* (London: A & C Black, updated annually). Another standard market guide for the United Kingdom, this is a directory for writers, artists, and playwrights; writers for film, radio, and television; photographers; and composers.

▸ *Writing and Publishing Books for Children in the 1990's: The Inside Story from the Editor's Desk* by Olga Litowinsky (New York: Walker, 1992).

Various market guides are published by Writer's Digest Books (Cincinnati, OH) and updated annually, including:

▸ *The Writer's Market*

▸ *Poet's Market*

▸ *Song Writer's Market*

▸ *Novel & Short Story Writer's Market*

▸ *Children's Writer's & Illustrator's Market* (with a special section of listings for young writers).

For more information, write to: Writer's Digest Books, 1507 Dana Avenue, Cincinnati, OH 45207, U.S.A.

CHAPTER SIX

Preparing Your Manuscript

THE CLOCK HAS JUST STRUCK SIX P.M. Jane, the fiction editor at Project X Publications, looks up at the clock and then back at the large pile of manuscripts sitting on her desk. She wants to at least have a glance at all of them before she leaves the office tonight.

She picks up the whole stack and moves over to a large conference table where she can lay them out one by one. Jane has worked as an editor for five years. She has learned how to weed the professionally written manuscripts from the unprofessional ones. She figures that if people who send in manuscripts haven't taken the time to prepare them properly, they probably haven't taken much care with their writing.

She starts sorting through the pile. The first submission has a one-page cover letter and a sample chapter. A quick glance shows that it is well-organized. It goes to the left side of the table – the potentials. The second submission has a five-page cover letter. On quick examination, the sample chapter is single-spaced and the type is so light that Jane has to squint to see it. She groans and wonders if writers ever think about how much editors have to read. She puts that submission to the right side of the table – the questionables.

Meanwhile, down the corridor from Jane, Rob, the nonfiction editor, is in his office looking at a large stack of nonfiction submissions. He quickly splits up the file into those submissions that have a cover letter stating how long the book will be and when it will be ready for publication, plus a well-organized book proposal with brief outlines of each chapter and a sample chapter. He is not happy to see full-length manuscripts with no book proposal. It means more work in trying to figure out if the book really has potential. He wonders if writers ever read the comments he puts in the *Market Guide* every year. He also wonders if writers ever think about what would make life easier for the editor.

One of the most important skills writers can learn is to be able to put themselves into the reader's shoes. Every time you submit a piece of writing – whether to a publisher, a magazine or newspaper editor, a contest judge, or whoever – *keep the reader in mind*. While you may be very clear about what your piece is about, to the reader your work is always new. It is information that has to be understood.

"Your audience is one single reader. I have found that sometimes it helps to pick out one person – a real person you know, or an imagined person, and write to that one."

John Steinbeck, author of THE GRAPES OF WRATH, winner of the Pulitzer Prize

General Guidelines

You can use these *general* guidelines to prepare your manuscript for a publisher, a contest, or anyone you are asking to critique your writing and give you feedback (see Chapter Eight). On pages 117–121, you'll find more specific suggestions for submitting a novel and a nonfiction book proposal. Some publishers have prepared guidelines they would like you to follow when submitting a manuscript. Ask them to send you copies of their guidelines.

- Double-space all manuscripts, except poetry. To double-space your text, either set the line spacing of your typewriter to the number 2, or use the double-space command on your word processing program.

- Make sure that you have used paragraphs. Don't submit short stories or articles that are all one paragraph. Paragraphs are natural breaks in your writing. If you don't know what paragraphs are, ask your English teacher or parents for help.

- If you have used dialogue in your story, make sure to start a new paragraph whenever a new person speaks. Enclose all dialogue in quotation marks.

- Make sure that each page is clearly numbered. Pages should be numbered in sequence from the beginning to the end of your manuscript.

- Keep your manuscript simple, neat, and clean. Although it may seem strange to your creative urge, what works best in publishing is simple black type on white pages. Focus your attention on making your work easy to read. Avoid drawing on your poems, scribbling in your margins, using bizarre stationery, or going wild with graphics and type fonts on your computer. Any art should be submitted on separate pieces of paper.

- Use good paper that can stand up to the test of being read a few times and passed around. Sixteen- to twenty-pound white bond paper works well.

- Make sure that your spelling is correct throughout. You can ask someone to proofread your work for you. If you use a spell checker on your computer, remember that these programs are not perfect. They just find the most common errors – and they can't tell when you've used the wrong word (such as "to" for "two" or "rein" for "rain").

- Make sure that your grammar is correct throughout.

- Avoid overusing lines, extra spaces, or symbols (such as ****) to mark breaks in a story or article. If your piece has too many breaks, you may need to split it up into chapters or sections with subtitles.

- Think of the front page as telling your readers everything they need to know: your name, address, telephone number, the word count of your piece, the date you are submitting it, the title, and the author (you).

- The last page of your manuscript should let readers know that they have reached the end of your piece. At the end of your manuscript, drop down two lines and center the words "The End." Or do what professional journalists do and use the number thirty (-30-).

- Use a paper clip or a long rubber band to hold your manuscript together. Don't staple or bind it.

An Incorrect First Page

```
                    SPLIT PEA SOUP
                          by
                  Christine Carriere
                          ↓

The setting for the whole dilemma was incredibly
inappropriate. Glittering chandeliers, probably plas-
tic, but I thought at the time they were crystal;
candlelit tables; embossed wallpaper, and hidden air
conditioners; not to mention exotic prices. You are
probably wondering what I was doing in such a place
alone. I had just been given a raise. After months
of careful planning, I had decided to celebrate.
I had ordered fish paté, and pecan pie for dessert.
It only cost $14.99; an amazing money-saver compared
to numerous $29.99's and $45.99's that were offered
for truffles and the like. Anyway, I was thinking
dark thoughts about the tardiness of my food when
I noticed a man two tables away from me wink sugges-
tively. "Ick!" I thought. "Half bald with wrinkles."
Even worse, he had a peculiar taste for red wine and
soup...split pea. He took a sip from his soup
spoon, swallowed, and smiled.
```

A Correct First Page

Christine Carriere   About 1,500 words

597 2nd St.   June 15, 1995

Centertown, MN 34567

(555) 232-7788

SPLIT PEA SOUP

by

Christine Carriere

The setting for the whole dilemma was incredibly
inappropriate. Glittering chandeliers, probably plas-
tic, but I thought at the time they were crystal;
candlelit tables; embossed wallpaper, and hidden air
conditioners; not to mention exotic prices.

You are probably wondering what I was doing in
such a place alone. I had just been given a raise.
After months of careful planning, I had decided to
celebrate. I had ordered fish paté, and pecan pie for
dessert. It only cost $14.99; an amazing money-saver
compared to numerous $29.99's and $45.99's that were
offered for truffles and the like.

A Correct Second Page

Carriere   SPLIT PEA SOUP   2

    Anyway, I was thinking dark thoughts about the tardiness of my food when I noticed a man two tables away from me wink suggestively.

    "Ick!" I thought. "Half bald with wrinkles."

    Even worse, he had a peculiar taste for red wine and soup...split pea. He took a sip from his soup spoon, swallowed, and smiled. Then he smiled even more widely and dipped his spoon again. Suddenly, he shrieked, drawing the attention of every customer in the restaurant. He banged his spoon wildly on his water glass.

Preparing Your Cover Letter

If you are submitting poems, short stories, articles, etc. for a contest, you don't need to send a cover letter. But if you are submitting any of your writing for normal publication, it is wise to send a cover letter.

A cover letter is like a regular letter. You write your name, address, telephone number, and date at the top. Then you write the name of the person you are sending it to, plus his or her address. Then begin your letter with "Dear Mr. or Ms." If you can't find the person's name, put "Editor."

Keep your letter brief and to the point. A cover letter should never be longer than one page. State what you are sending, why you are sending it, and how you see it fitting into their publication or publishing list.

A Correct Cover Letter

Christine Carriere

597 2nd St.

Centertown, MN 34567

(555) 232-7788

June 15, 1995

The Editor

Project X Publications

P.O. Box 69

Seattle, WA 45678

Dear Editor:

I have enclosed a short story, "Split Pea Soup," for consideration in your anthology for young adults.
I have read both your 1993 and 1994 anthologies, and feel this story would be a natural fit for your 1995 version.

Yours sincerely,

Christine Carriere

ENC: "Split Pea Soup," SASE

Preparing Your Envelope and SASE

You will need two envelopes that are both big enough to hold your manuscript. A Number 10 business envelope will work for manuscripts under four pages. Any manuscripts larger than that should be put into a 9" × 12" envelope. Your manuscript should slip out of the envelope at the other end, looking as clean and crisp as it did when you sent it off.

Address the first envelope to the person and publisher you are sending your manuscript to. Be sure to put your return address on the envelope. The second envelope, called an SASE (for Self-Addressed Stamped Envelope), is addressed to you and includes the publisher's return address. You need to put enough postage on it so your manuscript can be returned to you.

Always remember to include an SASE. It saves the person who receives your manuscript or inquiry the trouble of typing up an envelope and paying the postage. As you can imagine, the time and money involved in returning thousands of manuscripts would be tremendous. If you don't include an SASE, your submission package will probably not be returned to you, even if the publisher decides not to publish your work.

SAMPLE MAILING ENVELOPE

Christine Carriere
597 2nd St.
Centertown, MN 34567

U.S. Postage

The Editor
Project X Publications
P.O. Box 69
Seattle, WA 45678

Sample SASE

Project X Publications
P.O. Box 69
Seattle, WA 45678

U.S. Postage

Christine Carriere
597 2nd St.
Centertown, MN 34567

How to Submit a Novel

Once you have identified the publishers you want to send your novel to, read and re-read their entries in *The Writer's Market* or *Writer's Handbook* very carefully. Don't just send off copies of your novel. Most editors will specify if they would like to receive a brief synopsis (one-paragraph summary) along with one, two, or three sample chapters. Take your sample chapters from different parts of the book. You should always send the first chapter. Then choose one from the middle and one from the end.

Some editors like to receive manuscripts in their entirety. This is especially true for children's books. If the editor has not given specific instructions for what to submit, you can always telephone the editor's office and ask what the normal procedure is for submitting a manuscript. Be brief and polite.

To find out more about submitting your writing in the proper format, read:

- *The Writer's Digest Guide to Manuscript Formats* by Dian Dincin Buchman and Seli Groves (Cincinnati, OH: Writer's Digest Books, 1988).

- *How to Write Irresistible Query Letters* by Lisa Cool (Cincinnati, OH: Writer's Digest Books, 1990).

How to Submit a Nonfiction Book Proposal

A good nonfiction proposal contains the following five elements:

1. A letter about the book

2. A working chapter outline (defined below)

3. A summary of each chapter

4. One or more sample chapters, and

5. A marketing and competition summary.

1. A Letter about the Book

Tell how many pages you expect the book to be. Check libraries and bookstores to find out the typical nonfiction book lengths for the age group you are writing for (children, young adults, adults). You'll discover that while there is some flexibility with page counts, some types of books, especially children's books, have a certain number of pages they don't go above or below.

Tell when you expect to finish your manuscript, if it is not already completed. Usually, books are published twice a year – in the spring and the fall. You will need to have your manuscript to the publisher at least six months to a year before the expected publication date. Large publishers usually require even longer than that.

Tell what the book is about. Pretend that you are writing the copy for the book jacket or back cover. Read some book jackets or back covers to get the idea. Three or four very clear paragraphs will do.

2. A Working Chapter Outline

A working chapter outline is like a table of contents in a school report or book. You may find it helpful to examine the tables of contents in your favorite nonfiction books, or in nonfiction books dealing with the same topic you are writing about. You can also break down the chapters into subheads to give a clear idea of what your book will include.

Sample Working Chapter Outline

WORKING CHAPTER OUTLINE

by Janet E. Grant and Kristin J. Pedersen

Self-Image: It All Starts with Self-Esteem

The Domino Effect

1. Re-Inventing Your Self-Image
    - Teen #1's Story
    - Take Action

2. Acknowledgment
    - Teen #2's Story
    - Take Action

3. Balance and Focus
    - Teen #3's Story
    - Take Action

4. Confidentiality and Privacy
    - Teen #4's Story
    - Take Action

5. Partnership and Accomplishment
    - Teen #5's Story
    - Take Action

Coaching

Recommended Reading

3. A Summary of Each Chapter

Write one or two paragraphs about the main points in each chapter. Be very concise but precise. This may require a lot of writing and rewriting.

SAMPLE CHAPTER SUMMARY

SUMMARY: CHAPTER FIVE

Partnership and Accomplishment

Females thrive on developing successful relation-
ships. Yet most environments encourage competition
between females, rather than learning how to support
each other. In order to survive the 21st century,
young females need to learn how to create partner-
ships, not only with other young women and men, but
with the adults in their lives.

Tina's Story: I have a dream...I have a vision.
Making it happen through a network of support with
your own age group. The difference between giving
advice and coaching.

Take Action: Networking.

---

4. One or More Sample Chapters

Submit the best chapter you have, or the one you think best conveys what your book is about and how you will write it. Follow all of the general guidelines for preparing a manuscript on pages 109–110.

5. A Marketing and Competition Summary

This is a one- or two-page document that explains why you think the book will sell and why you are the best person to write it. It should also list any other books that are similar to yours and why you think yours is different from and better than the others.

Manuscript Submission Checklist

Are you ready to submit your manuscript? Write the following checklist in your Writer's Notebook, then check off each part you have completed.

___ A partial or complete publishable manuscript, checked to make sure that the grammar and spelling are correct

___ An envelope addressed to the editor

___ An SASE so the publisher can return your manuscript if necessary

___ A cover letter, checked to make sure that the publisher's name and address are correct.

For a novel:

___ A synopsis

___ Sample chapter(s).

For a work of nonfiction:

___ A letter about the book

___ A working chapter outline

__ A summary of each chapter

__ One or more sample chapters

__ A marketing and competition summary.

Optional:

__ A biographical description ("bio sheet"). See the next Writer's Notebook exercise.

WRITER'S NOTEBOOK

Preparing Your Bio Sheet

Some publishers include "About the Author" descriptions in their books. (There's one on pages 174–175 of this book.) Also, publishers like to have author descriptions on hand for publicity purposes. A description of your interests, writing accomplishments, and background may help to pique an editor's interest in your work.

Rather than writing up the same information every time you submit a manuscript or an idea, it saves time to have a standard "bio sheet" on hand to photocopy or print out and enclose with your submissions. Use your Writer's Notebook to prepare a rough draft of your bio sheet. Then type it neatly or enter it into your computer. Use black ink on white paper.

Your bio sheet should include:

- your name, home address, and telephone number

- the name, address, and telephone number of your school or college

- any clubs, organizations, etc. you belong to

- a list of your published works

- any special awards you have received or experiences you have had

- a list of magazines or newspapers you write for
- any writing workshops you have attended
- any speeches or talks you have given, classes you have taught, or workshops you have led.

Keep your bio sheet current. Update it whenever you publish something new, receive a new award, or attend a workshop.

You might also want to attach a good, current black-and-white photograph of yourself to your bio sheet.

How to Keep a Publication Record

You will want to keep track of where and when you send out your manuscripts so you can follow up on any replies you receive from publishers, or write to publishers who have had your manuscripts for a very long time (six months or longer) without responding to you.

An easy way to keep a publication record is to write the information on 3" × 5" cards and file them in a box. Make a card for each manuscript you send out. Record the title of your story, novel, proposal, or article, then list the publisher(s) you send it to. Be sure to write the date(s) you sent it. Record any response(s) you receive.

You'll find an example of a filled-out card on page 124.

SAMPLE PUBLICATION RECORD

Record of Submission: Year 1995

Title: "Split Pea Soup"

Date Sent: June 15, 1995

Sent to: Project X Publications

Their Reply: Accepted!

Date: August 12, 1995

Your Money and Your Publishing Rights

WHEN YOU ARE YOUNG, you experience a real sense of inner satisfaction with the first money you earn from any job or work you do. At the beginning of your writing career, the joy of being published and making some extra pocket money will be immensely satisfying to you.

You may find that a short story of yours has been chosen for an anthology and you are $200 richer. Or your novel has just won a $500 prize. Or you have sold three nonfiction articles to various magazines for a total of $150. Or your nonfiction book has won a national contest and a scholarship for you.

There are authors who have made millions of dollars from their books…and authors who have lived in poverty for most of their lives. In between are authors who have made a comfortable living from their writing. Unless you have a private income (like an inheritance), you will need to get a full-time job and pursue your writing in your spare time until you become successful. (The reading you did for the Writer's Notebook exercise in Chapter One, "An Afternoon with Your Favorite Authors," may have given you some ideas about working and writing after completing school.)

As you move from earning extra pocket money from your writing, to wanting to earn a good part-time income, to wanting to earn a good full-time income, your financial skills will need to become increasingly better. Most important, you need to understand *now* that with a bit of foresight and planning, you can avoid the two most common financial mistakes writers make: overspending the money you earn, and not using your financial skills to become a successful writer.

Handling money and understanding publishing contracts are two skills that will be a lifetime in the making. I think even young writers should have a *very basic* understanding of how writers are paid. I say "basic" because every writer is paid differently, depending on what they write, how much they write, who they publish with, how well they are known, etc. You should also have a *very basic* understanding of publishing contracts, if you are at the stage in your writing when you are submitting full-length manuscripts to publishers.

When you are an adult, you may choose to delegate these tasks to an accountant, a financial planner, a lawyer, and/or an agent (someone who acts on your behalf with publishers). Or you may decide to handle them yourself. I don't know which route you will take, since we all come from different backgrounds and have different interests and abilities. Some of us like playing with numbers, and some of us don't.

The information in this chapter is divided into three parts.

- The first part, "How Writers Get Paid," answers the most common questions young writers have about how much to expect for a piece of writing, when payment occurs, and other issues concerning money. The examples involve very simple multiplication, division, and percentages.

- The second part, "Budgets," is meant for slightly older young writers (ages 16 and up).

- The third part, "Your Rights and Your Contract," describes various rights that you as a writer will negotiate with your editor or publisher and introduces the complex subject of book publishing contracts.

Depending on your age and your interests, you may want to read the first part now and leave the second and third parts for later. Just make a note in your Writer's Notebook to come back to these parts in a few years or whenever you feel ready.

How Writers Get Paid

Writers are usually paid for their writing in one of five ways, and sometimes a combination of two or more:

- in free copies
- by the word
- with a flat fee
- with royalties, and/or
- with an advance.

Free Copies

Some smaller magazines and book publishers may not pay you any money at all for publishing your writing. Instead, they will send you free copies of the magazine your writing appears in, or free copies of your book.

If you are just starting out as a writer, being paid in free copies isn't unusual, and it isn't necessarily a bad thing. Some small magazines and book publishers can't afford to pay their writers very much, if at all. The copies make good samples of your writing to show to other editors. Be sure to keep updating the list of published works on your bio sheet (see pages 122–123).

If you have already published your writing in other places, an offer to be paid in free copies isn't so terrific. Whether you accept will depend on the publication and how much you want your work to appear there.

By the Word

Payment by the word – or *per word*, in professional language – most often applies to magazine writing. When you send away for a magazine's guidelines, they should include a description of their payment terms: how much they pay, when they pay, and what rights they buy (discussed on page 136).

For example, imagine that you have written a 300-word article on a championship baseball game for your local newspaper. They pay 7 cents per word, so your 300-word article will earn you $21.

When can you expect your check? Most magazines and newspapers pay *on acceptance* or *on publication.* "On acceptance" means that they will send you a check as soon as they accept your article, no matter when they plan to publish it. "On publication" means that they will send you a check when your article is published. In other words, if you submit an article to a magazine in January and the editor decides to publish it in the June issue, you won't receive payment until June. (Writers learn quickly that they sometimes have to wait a long time to get paid.)

Flat Fee

Another common way magazines pay is with a flat fee – a fixed amount of money for a certain type of writing, no matter how long it is. This type of payment may apply to short stories, single poems, and articles. It even applies to certain books.

For example, imagine that you have written a personal essay for a youth magazine. Their guidelines state that they pay a flat fee of $25. Once again, this may be paid on acceptance or on publication. Check the guidelines or ask.

Royalties

Royalties are the most complicated way to get paid, but they can sometimes be the most financially rewarding. If you don't understand this section right away, ask your parents or teachers for help. (Please don't feel embarrassed if you don't understand. Royalties are a mystery to many adult authors.)

To put it simply, a royalty is a percentage of your book's selling price that is paid to you, the author. The royalty you receive depends on how many copies of your book are sold. *It's important to understand that the selling price may not always be the price printed on the cover of your book.* For example, bookstores buy books for less than the cover price, sell them for the cover price, and keep the difference. (They need to make a profit, too.)

Royalty rates differ from publisher to publisher. They may depend on the type of book being published (hardcover, trade paperback, and mass market paperback), how many books are printed, the size of the potential audience, and the country of publication. The average royalty percentage range is anywhere from 5%–15%. Royalties are usually paid once a year or twice a year (every six months). They come with a *royalty statement* which tells you how many of your books have been sold and may also include other interesting information.

For example, imagine that you have written a young adult novel for a major publisher. Your book sells for $4.95. (Let's use the cover price for this example, since this makes the math easier to do.) You have agreed to receive a 10% royalty on each book sold. The publisher has agreed to send you a royalty statement and a check every six months.

How much money will you receive for each book sold? Take the cover price ($4.95) and multiply it by 10% (.10). The answer is .495, or just under 50 cents. This is the basic royalty that you, the author, will receive for each book sold.

- Your first royalty statement tells you that your book sold 500 copies in the first six months after publication. Your royalty is .495 × 500, or $250. Along with your royalty statement is a check for that amount.

- Six months later, your second royalty statement arrives. Your book has sold 1,000 more copies. Your royalty is .495 × 1,000, or $500.

- Six months later, your third royalty statement arrives. Your book has sold 500 more copies. Your royalty is .495 × 500, or $250. So far, you have made $1,000 in royalties.

Now imagine that over the course of five years, your book sells 5,000 copies. You earn a total of $2,500 in royalties. During that time, neither you nor your publisher could have predicted exactly how many of your books would sell or how much in royalties you would earn.

The more you write, and the more you publish, the better you will get at making good "guesstimates" of future royalties. But you have to be prepared for the worst *and* the best. Very few writers can live off of royalties alone. (See "More Sources of Income for Writers" on pages 130–131.)

Advance

Along with royalties, you might be paid an advance for your book. An advance is money the publisher pays to you out of your *potential* royalties. It's called an advance because you receive it "in advance" of any actual royalties, and it is charged against future royalties. In other words, an advance now will mean lower royalties (or no royalties) until your advance has all been earned by sales of your book. For example, if your young adult novel earns $2,500 in royalties during the first five years it is in print, but you received a $2,500 advance, you won't receive any royalties until the sixth year.

It might help to think of an advance like this: You need to pay for a new pair of skates out of your allowance money. There is a skating competition scheduled for this Friday. You want your new skates in time for the competition, but you need three weeks' worth of allowance money to buy them. You ask your parents for an advance on your allowance. They grant your request and give you the money. For the next three weeks, you don't receive an allowance, because you are earning the advance your parents gave you.

If you are writing a nonfiction book, you may need an advance to cover your costs while you are writing. If you have written a novel, you may need an advance so you have some money between the time your manuscript is accepted and the time you receive your first royalty payment, which can be as long as two years away. Typically, a book gets *signed* (accepted) one year and published the next, with royalty checks starting the following year (if sales exceed the advance).

Obviously, an advance means different things to different authors, depending on how much money they have in the bank, whether they have a job that covers their living costs, and so on. Advances, like royalties, vary according to the type of book you are writing, the publisher, and the country you are living in. If you are offered a contract, you will want to contact a local professional writing organization and get some guidance on how much of an advance to ask for.

More Sources of Income for Writers

Royalties and advances are just two possible sources of income for a writer. Most authors make money from many different types of activities. These might include:

- grants from government or private agencies
- prizes or awards for contests or competitions
- reproduction or reprint agreements (payment for permission to reproduce your writing or portions of your writing for use in schools, libraries, etc.)
- freelance assignments (for magazines, newspapers, book reviews, etc.)
- speaking at conferences
- leading workshops
- public readings (at schools, libraries, conferences, etc.)
- public lending rights (in Canada, England, Europe, and Australia, writers are paid for the use of their books in libraries).

Most writers also have other paying jobs, which may or may not be related to their writing.

"Money to a writer is time to write."
Frank Herbert, author of DUNE

RECOMMENDED READING

▸ *How to Become a Teenage Millionaire* by Todd Temple (Nashville: Thomas Nelson, Inc., 1991). Written for young adults, this is a very humorous book, with easy-to-apply tips and techniques.

▸ *Moneylove: How to Get the Money You Deserve for Whatever You Want* by Jerry Gillies (New York: Warner, 1988). Written for adults, but very easy to read.

Budgets

Training in how to manage money is probably one of the most over-looked parts of our education. Unless you are fortunate to have parents who are teaching you about money management, budgeting, and financial planning, or unless you are learning it in school, this will be a new area for you. Those of you who have already mastered budgets (I know you are out there; I read about you in *Computing* magazine) can speed through this section.

The information presented here is a bit more complicated than what you have read in other parts of this book. To understand it, you will need to know how to do basic math. You can use a calculator or a computer spreadsheet program. Make sure that you understand each section before moving on to the next. If you come across something you don't understand, ask your parents or a teacher to help you.

Give yourself plenty of time to complete this section. Don't rush through it. You can do one step at a time.

Writing a Budget

A personal financial plan includes a *budget, short-term goals,* and *long-term goals.* A budget includes *income, expenses,* and *savings.*

- Your income is the money you have coming in from your part-time job, allowance, or special gifts of money.

- Expenses are money you pay out, either regularly or occasionally.

- Regular expenses are called *fixed expenses.* After high school or college, one of your largest fixed expenses will probably be rent. Fixed expenses also include food, electricity, telephone, savings, and insurance.

- Occasional expenses are called *flexible expenses.* These can be large or small. Your flexible expenses might include a new version of a computer program you use, new clothes, compact discs or cassettes, books, magazines, movies, memberships, restaurant meals, and gifts.

You might not consider savings to be a fixed expense, but you should. That way, you are sure to save something from every paycheck, royalty check, or gift of money. You are probably already saving for college or to move out on your own when you graduate from school and get a full-time job.

There is another important reason for having a separate savings account that may not have crossed your mind. If you want to purchase a major item that involves taking out a bank loan, you will be able to get a loan and good interest terms if you can secure the loan with a healthy savings account. For example, if you wanted to borrow $3,000 to buy a used car, you should have at least $1,000 in a savings account.

Catriona's Budget

Catriona is 16 years old. She works part-time at a local bookstore – 10 hours per week. She makes $5 an hour. Her monthly income from her job is $200. She also gets a $10 allowance from her parents.

Currently, Catriona spends most of her income on books and the occasional compact disc. She is saving $50 per month for college. Because she wants to get better control over her money, she decides to do a budget. She lists her income and expenses along the left-hand side of a page. Then she creates three columns at the top: Estimate, Target, and Actual.

Column 1: Estimate. First, Catriona tries to figure out what happened to the money she earned last month. She is surprised to see that there is $60 she cannot account for. She spent the whole $210 she earned from her job and her allowance, but her estimates only add up to $150.

Column 2: Target. Before completing this column, Catriona considers her short-term and long-term goals. She is already saving money for college. She also wants to save money for a second-hand computer, which will cost $600. And she wants to attend a writing workshop, which will cost $100. She increases her savings to include these goals – and reduces the amount of money she will spend on compact discs, clothes, and books.

Column 3: Actual. Catriona saves her receipts for the next month and totals them at the end of the month. She sees that she has kept to her budget, with one exception: There weren't any CD's that interested her that month, so she put the extra $25 into her computer savings account.

ONE-MONTH BUDGET

	Column 1 Estimate	Column 2 Target	Column 3 Actual
Income			
Allowance	$ 10.00	$ 10.00	$ 10.00
Job	$ 200.00	$ 200.00	$ 200.00
Gifts	$ 0.00	$ 0.00	$ 0.00
Total Income	$ 210.00	$ 210.00	$ 210.00
Expenses			
Fixed			
Savings (College)	$ 50.00	$ 50.00	$ 50.00
Savings (Workshop)	$ 0.00	$ 25.00	$ 25.00
Savings (Computer)	$ 0.00	$ 25.00	$ 50.00
Flexible			
Clothes	$ 50.00	$ 25.00	$ 25.00
Books	$ 50.00	$ 25.00	$ 25.00
CDS	?	$ 25.00	$ 0.00
Entertainment	?	$ 25.00	$ 25.00
Gifts	?	$ 10.00	$ 10.00
Total Expenses	$ 150.00	$ 210.00	$ 210.00

Can You Afford a Computer?

If you don't already have a computer and a modem, you will want to save money to buy them. These are among the most important purchases a writer can plan for and make.

When you have a computer with a word processing program, you don't need to re-write (or re-type) everything from scratch as soon as you make one mistake. A spreadsheet program can keep your budget and do all the math for you. A modem can connect you to on-line services and the Internet – valuable sources of information for research and fact-finding (and excellent ways to connect with other writers through chat groups and news groups).

Computers and modems don't need to be costly purchases. Some excellent second-hand computers and modems can be purchased for a fraction of their original prices.

Write Your Own Budget

Using Catriona's budget as a guide, write your own budget in your Writer's Notebook. Complete the Estimate column as best you can, using your past month's expenses as a guide. You may be surprised, as Catriona was (and many other people are), to discover that there is a sum of money you can't account for.

Complete the Target column with the budget you would like to follow for the next month. Be sure to include any short-term goals. Remember to write in a figure for your savings account.

Write the name of the next month on an envelope. During that month, file all of your receipts in the envelope. At the end of the month, complete the Actual column on your budget. How did you do? Are there any changes that need to be made to the Target column for your budget to work for you?

Why should you do this exercise? Running out of your allowance in the middle of the week may not be a big issue right now, but it may be a sign of poor planning. This can lead to dangerous spending habits in the future, when you are responsible for all of your expenses. A budget can help you to spend your money on what you really want. It can keep you from throwing your money away on things you don't really want or need. Once you know where your money is going, it will be easier to cover any regular expenses and put money toward your short- and long-term goals.

Your Rights and Your Contract

Copyright

One of the first words to learn regarding your rights as a writer is *copyright*. When you hold the copyright for a piece of writing, it means that you *own* your writing. A copyright is indicated by the © symbol. You can copyright an original piece of writing simply by putting this notice on the front page (some writers put it on every page):

Copyright © [Year] by [Your Name].

Copyright laws vary from country to country. In the United States, written works are copyrighted for the lifetime of the author plus 50 years after his or her death, unless the author sells the copyright.

Selling your copyright is usually the *last* thing you want to do. If a certain publisher is asking you to give up your copyright, you have two choices: look for another place to publish your book or article, or talk to a professional writing association and see if you have any other options.

When you write for a magazine, they will usually buy one of two types of rights (not your copyright): *First Serial Rights* or *Second Serial Rights*. First Serial Rights means that the magazine wants the right to publish your article for the first time. Second Serial Rights means that the magazine wants the right to publish it again, after it has appeared in another magazine.

First and Second Serial Rights also apply to books. First Serial Rights means that a publisher wants the right to publish an excerpt from your book in a magazine before the book comes out. Second Serial Rights means that the publisher wants to excerpt from your book after it comes out.

Contracts

When you submit a manuscript to a publisher, and the publisher accepts it, you will be asked to sign a *contract* giving the publisher the right to publish your work. A contract is a complex legal document. In most cases, you will receive the publisher's "standard" contract. Unfortunately for the beginning writer, no two publishers have the same standard contract, and if you have no experience in negotiating or understanding legal documents, you are not in a good bargaining position. Fortunately for the beginning writer, almost all professional writing organizations in most countries around the world have some guidelines for understanding contracts. Even if you are exceptionally bright and used to handling problems, the legal implications of every clause in a contract can take months (if not years) to really understand if you try to do it all yourself. Since contracts can run anywhere from 5–25 pages and even longer, the best advice I can give you is to order a set of guidelines from your local writing organization – now.

If you get an offer of a contract on a book, play, book of poems, or anything you have written, you will want to contact the relevant writing organization in your country. On pages 158–159, you'll find lists of writing organizations for several countries. Meanwhile, the general guidelines that follow will give you some idea of what to watch for and what to do.

General Contract Guidelines

Almost all beginning writers (unless they come from a family of bankers or lawyers) think that a contract is written in stone. In fact, most contracts can be negotiated, and some changes can be made. You especially want to make sure that you understand what money you can make from your published writing and what subsidiary rights you will have a say in.

Countless beginning writers have signed contracts in a rush, only to find at a later date that their contracts did not contain the terms the authors really wanted. When you receive a contract, take a deep breath, because you will have to switch from your creative hat to your business hat. Then follow these steps.

1. **Read the contract.** Read every word. If you are handed your contract in the editor's office, never sign it then and there. Instead, take it home. It may take a week or two (or longer) to fully understand, negotiate, and sign your contract. Don't rush this process because you are excited. (In most countries, if you are under 18, your parents will need to sign the contract with you. Make sure that they read it as carefully as you do.)

2. **Take out the guide to contracts you received from your local or national writing organization.** Read the guide and compare it to the contract you have been offered. Mark any clauses in your contract that are okay with a check. Mark anything (and I mean *anything*) you have a question about with a question mark.

3. **Call the person on staff at the publishing house who is in charge of contracts.** He or she will help you to understand the clauses you are not clear about. (Before placing the call, make sure that you have read your contract carefully and have learned everything you can about publishing contracts.)

4. **Prepare a list of what you really want in your contract.** This might include royalty rates, advance amounts, specific rights, etc. If you decide that you must negotiate a better contract, be polite and diplomatic in your negotiations. Listen carefully to the publisher's side in case you have misread a clause. Then calmly explain what you want and why. Remember that a good relationship with your publisher is crucial. On the other hand, you need to make sure that everything is in writing, in case the publishing house gets sold at some point in the future, and the relationship you had with the original publisher comes to an end.

IMPORTANT!

Never sign a book contract without first talking to a staff person in a professional writing organization, your lawyer, or your agent. (If you have an agent, he or she will handle the contract negotiations for you, after talking with you to find out what you want. If you have a lawyer, make sure that he or she specializes in "Intellectual Property" law.) One of the most important things to remember is not to suffer in silence. If you can't figure out what a clause in a contract means, or you've submitted a piece of writing and have never been paid properly for it, or someone has taken over the copyright on something you have written, *immediately* get in touch with one of the professional writing organizations listed on pages 158–159.

READING CHALLENGE

To find out more about contracts, read:

▸ *Answers to Some Questions about Contracts,* available from The Society of Children's Book Writers and Illustrators, 22736 Vanowen Street, Suite 106, West Hills, CA 91307, U.S.A.

▸ *Help Yourself to a Better Contract,* available from The Writers' Union of Canada, 24 Ryerson Avenue, Toronto, Ontario, M5T 2P3, Canada.

CHAPTER EIGHT

Connecting with the Writing Community

AN INTEREST IN WRITING transcends all of the normal age barriers. At the International Young Authors' Camp, 11-year-olds mixed naturally with 17-year-olds. At social functions with adult author groups, 20-year-olds mix naturally with 80-year-olds.

Having conversations with people about things we find interesting is vital for our development. While we are engaged in conversations, all sorts of new possibilities can emerge. A chance comment to a friend about the fact that you want to find a writing class may turn up the contact name you've been looking for. A question to your local book-store owner or teacher about needing more interesting books may take you to a section or shelf of books you have previously overlooked.

The conversations you have – not only with other people, but also with yourself – can be among the most important tools for becoming a writer. In conversations, you make promises to yourself to do certain things by a certain time. In conversations, you make requests of people (for example, you ask someone to help you find an address). In con-versations, you make declarations – like "I am a writer" – which serve as launching pads for future actions.

How and Where to Find Other Writers

While you may have to pull out some of your top-notch sleuthing skills to find other young writers, the reward of a new friend (or friends) who loves reading and writing as much as you do is well worth it. I say "pull out your sleuthing skills" because you may have to pick up the phone or speak face-to-face to people you've never dreamed of speaking to before. You may have to dig for information.

A writing club may already exist at your school, at another local school, at your local library, or at a bookstore. If you can't find a writing club, you may have to start your own. Young writers have found friends at local writing clubs, at drama workshops, and by working part-time in libraries or bookstores. Other ways young writers find each other include:

- by attending a young writers' workshop
- by working on a school or community newspaper
- by writing for a pen pal through special young authors' magazines
- by asking an English teacher, journalism teacher, drama teacher, or librarian if he or she knows of other young writers in the school. (You may not know these people yet because they are not in your class or your grade.)

There are also opportunities to reach out and connect in the adult writing community. If you can show that you are writing regularly and that you enjoy talking with and being around adults, you may want to approach a local writing group. Find out who is responsible for introducing new members. Contact that person, then explain what you are writing and what you feel you could contribute to the group. You may not have to mention your age at all. I know plenty of 14-year-olds who can hold their own in discussions with adults. If this is the only way you can get in touch with other writers, try it out. You may feel at home right away, or you may need to attend a couple of meetings before you are comfortable.

The famous British actor and director, Kenneth Branagh, reflects on his experience as a teenager summoning up courage to join a local theater group: "I watched as people filed in and simply prayed that some kindly figure would walk across and say, 'Hello, you must be the hugely talented youngster we've been expecting. I'll look after you and make sure you don't feel utterly ridiculous and stupid. Come with me.' It didn't happen. I simply got cold and walked home."

Where can you find out about adult organizations? Ask at your library or bookstore. Try the phone book. Write to the organization of professional writers closest to you. Look for established organizations. For example, The Loft in Minneapolis, Minnesota, offers classes, sponsors readings, and provides all kinds of support for the local writing community. For more information, write to:

- The Loft: A Place for Writing and Literature, 66 Malcolm Avenue SE, Minneapolis, MN 55414, U.S.A.

In Great Britain, there are a couple of places where young writers (usually ages 16 and over) can go to write and get feedback on their work alongside adult authors:

- The Arvon Foundation, Totleigh Barton, Sheepwash, Beaworthy, Devon EX221 5NS, England.
- Fen Farm, 10 Angel Hill, Bury St. Edmunds, Suffolk 1P33 1UZ, England.

Plus, in each regional arts council there is a Literature Officer and a Theatre Officer, who advise young writers on local workshops as well as authors living in their area.

In London, there is a well-known theater group that encourages young playwrights:

- The Royal Court Young People's Theatre, 309 Portobello Road, London W10 5TD, England.

"Any writer, and especially the talented writer, needs an audience. The more immediate that audience is, the better for him because it stimulates him in his work; he gets a better view of himself and running criticism."

Truman Capote, author of BREAKFAST AT TIFFANY'S

Working with Other Young Writers

All writers have their own unique gifts to bring to the world. Given that writers come from different backgrounds and different schools, all writers (young and old) are at a different stage with their writing. It helps as you enter the world of writing to forget about grades and competing with each other. Instead, keep your focus on your writing.

If you are working on a picture book for a contest, there is not much point in worrying about whether your friend Angie, who is getting a short story published, is a better writer than you are. Even if your friend Mark is also working on a picture book for the same contest, you will find that supporting each other to write the best book possible will be far more helpful and inspiring. This may or may not mean reading each other's manuscript. It may mean simply celebrating together once your entries are in the mail. You'll know, based on your friendship, what is the best way to support each other.

The real power in friendship is looking for what you can contribute to each other without keeping score. Does Angie need encouragement to start her next short story? Does Mark need some encouragement to spend time at home writing tonight? Does Trudi need to borrow your book on developing plots in science fiction?

Professional authors focus on creating the best work possible. They form special friendships with other writers that last for years and are a source of inspiration.

Working with Other Artists

Other artists are also potential friends for young writers. Do you know any painters, photographers, or dancers? If you write short stories, do you know any poets or playwrights? Why not start a group in which artists of different disciplines meet and share their ideas? Artists around the world have learned that this can offer tremendous benefits for everyone.

From about 1904 through about 1939, "The Bloomsbury Group" met every Thursday night in Bloomsbury Square, London. The group consisted of John Maynard Keynes (economist), Virginia Woolf (novelist, short story writer, and autobiographer), Leonard Woolf (Virginia's husband and a political scientist), Lytton Strachey (biographer),

E.M. Forster (novelist), Vita Sackville-West (poet and novelist), and Roger Fry (painter). Some of the visitors to the group included T.S. Eliot and Bertrand Russell.

From the 1920s to the 1940s, a group of writers met informally in the dining room of the Algonquin Hotel in New York. The "Algonquin Round Table," as they were called, brought George S. Kaufman (playwright), Dorothy Parker (short-story writer), Robert Benchley (humorist and drama critic), Alexander Woollcott (theater critic and radio show host), Harpo Marx (member of the Marx Brothers comedy team), and others together for wit, merriment, and conversation about writing.

If you decide to meet only with writers, be sure to include people who write in many different genres. If you write short stories, find a playwright. If you're a poet, find a novelist or nonfiction writer.

Getting Other Kinds of Help

Most young writers are incredibly independent and self-sufficient. As you read through the following suggestions, keep in mind that these might be areas that your friends or parents can help you with. Your family members or friends who are not writers, and therefore may feel they don't have much to offer in helping you to become a writer, may be thrilled to assist you with one or more of these.

Design Your Writing Room

First of all, you need a place to go where you can think...dream... imagine...and *write*.

One of the things you might like to start doing right now is designing your writing room. Or, if you don't have a whole room to yourself, set up a writing corner or other special place in your home.

Use your writing room to inspire you. You may want to put up pictures or posters of a specific topic or setting you are using in a current story. I tend to like white walls and fresh, colorful flowers; they help me to keep the visual shape and structure of a book clear in my mind. My friend, author and illustrator Mark Thurman, has a skeleton in his workroom! Use anything that makes you feel like writing.

When you have an idea you care about strongly enough to want to write about it, try storing everything you find related to your idea in a special colored three-ring binder. I use different colors – for example, blue for nonfiction and pink for fiction. I always find it a great help to visualize a book as completed. I usually put a favorite comic strip or cartoon on the front cover to inspire me.

You can use file folders to hold brochures and other items that won't fit into a three-ring binder. A small filing cabinet or a set of wire baskets is also useful for organizing your materials.

Be environmentally friendly. Use both sides of your paper. Have two waste baskets in your writing room: one for paper to be recycled, and one for things that can't be recycled.

"A writer needs certain conditions in which to work and create art. She needs a piece of time; a peace of mind; a quiet place; and a private life."

Margaret Walker in THE WRITER ON HER WORK

Build a Personal Library

Start your own unique library of books. You may want to collect autographed books by your favorite authors. Or collect second-hand books or rare books. Remember, buying books supports the industry you wish to enter.

Get subscriptions to magazines you are interested in being published with. (Read copies at the library first if you are not familiar with them.)

Good books are as necessary to a writer as water is to a fish. Most young writers who are serious about writing soon realize the need to supplement the reading they do for school subjects. Nothing is more frustrating than having time to read and not having any good books close at hand. If you live in a city where there are many bookstores, or you have a bookstore in your community with a good owner, or if you have a good used-books store nearby, you are very fortunate. Also, libraries often have used-books sales.

Most young writers are eager for new books to read. You are probably on the lookout for books that challenge your beliefs; books with characters that transport you to another place or time; books that teach you about humankind as it was 100, 200, or 2,000 years ago; books that grapple with issues fundamental to being human. There are many, many good books available. The trick is knowing the titles, the authors, and where to find them.

Try reading some of the classics – Plato, Tolstoy, George Eliot. Classics have been treasured for years (in some cases, hundreds of years) because they are so astoundingly good that people don't want to forget them. You may want to consider buying some classics for your home library. (An easy way to find classics in the English language is to look for books with the Penguin or Signet Classics label.)

"A good writer needs a sense of the history
of literature to be successful as a writer, and
you need to read some Dickens, some Dostoyevsky,
some Melville, and other great classics –
because they are part of our world consciousness,
and the good writers tap into the
world consciousness when they create."

James Kisner, author of QUAGMIRE

Search for books in your particular genre, and preferably from a variety of cultures. Ask the bookstore owner or clerk if there are any new books in your favorite genre. You can also ask them to help you find books about writing. Bookstore owners buy books that they feel their general clientele will buy, and if you are looking for a particular title, you may not find it. Ask someone on staff to order it for you.

Be ready to give the title of the book, the author, the publisher, and the place and year it was published. Or, if the bookstore won't do special orders, you can call the publisher and order the book directly. While you are on the telephone, you may want to request a copy of their current catalog so you can see if they offer other books that might be of interest to you.

For birthdays or other special days when you receive presents, you may want to ask for unusual dictionaries, reference books, and anthologies that are normally out of your price range.

A Library of Classics

The purpose of this exercise is to encourage you to read the classics and start building your own library of classics.

Three of my favorite classics are:

- *The Red and the Black* by Stendhal
- *Madame Bovary* by Gustave Flaubert
- *Silas Marner* by George Eliot.

Set aside some time to read one of these titles. Then explore other classics and come up with your own three favorites. List them in your Writer's Notebook. Compare your favorites with a friend's favorites. Think about questions like these, and jot down your thoughts in your notebook:

- What interested you about a particular book?
- What was fascinating about the period of time the book was written in?
- Do good books really seem timeless? For example, do books written decades or centuries ago portray some of the same problems people have today?

Schedule Writing Time

If you have come up with your own writing timetable (see pages 62–64), share it with your parents. See if they will support you in working to meet your timetable. For example, if you find that you write best in the evening, you might ask if you can do the morning chores rather than the evening chores. Or, if you have a heavy homework burden and you can't see how to fit two hours of writing into a normal week, ask your parents what they would do. Perhaps they will see a solution where you can't.

Getting Support from Your Family

Thankfully, writing appears to be one of those careers that parents can't push their children towards. One of the nice things about writing is that it really depends on *your* initiative and talent. That is also what makes it so satisfying to actually succeed as a writer! At the same time, your parents can be a great help to you as you begin and continue your writing career.

I must admit that I never made many requests of my parents or relatives with respect to my writing. I simply wasn't very clear on how they could help. As I have worked with young writers and their parents over the years, I have developed a list of things young writers can do with their parents or other relatives. Read through them and think about any that appeal to you. Would these work with your parents or other relatives? Try them and see. Your family may turn out to be your biggest supporters.

Find Artistic Relatives

Ask your parents if you have any relatives that are working in or have a strong love of the arts. You may be surprised to learn that there is someone in your family besides you (an uncle? an older cousin?) who shares your love of books and writing. If he or she lives in another country, you can always write letters and swap stories and articles.

While I was at Sussex University in England, I was only miles away from my aunt, a syndicated columnist; my cousin, a playwright; my uncle, a journalist; and my cousin-in-law, an independent documentary producer. But as I had grown up in Canada and I hadn't really settled on a career in writing, it never even occurred to me to think of talking to them until I was much older.

If you don't have any artistic relations, perhaps your parents (or teachers) have a friend who is interested in being a mentor. For more on mentors, see page 151.

Attend Author Readings Together

If one (or more) of your relatives shares your interest in writing, you can go to author readings together. Readings at public libraries and bookstores are usually free. Readings at other places may charge small entrance fees.

A reading is a great way to meet an author and hear about his or her experiences. If you are building a library (or collection) of auto-graphed books, the author's books are usually for sale at the event.

I'll never forget a reading at Harbourfront in Toronto, Canada, where I chanced upon the first-ever public reading by Pat Conroy, author of *Prince of Tides*. I must admit that I didn't even know who he was, and I hadn't yet read the book. But he was so funny he had us rolling in the aisles, and because he had never done a reading before, he went way over the 20 minutes mark and regaled us for nearly an hour and a half! Readings can be one of those special events that stay in your memory for a lifetime.

Find Professional Coaching

Your parents may be willing to help you find writing workshops, or even a writer who is willing to coach you on an individual basis. They may be happy to send you to a summer writing camp or even help you put together the money to attend one – especially if there is nothing else available locally that can help you improve your writing during the year.

Getting Feedback on Your Writing

Along with praise and support, honest, constructive criticism is extremely important to young writers. Following are some ways you can get the feedback you need.

Find a Mentor

Derek Schraner, a young writer, remembers: "For most of my life I have dreamed of becoming a writer. In my teenage years, I gazed upon the likes of Gordon Korman and Lee J. Hindle (both had major publishing success as teenagers) with considerable admiration.... Oh, sure, I had a small handful of teachers along the way who urged me to continue, and my parents have always stood by my ideals, but nothing *big* happened. You probably know what I mean. I'm talking about the talent scout who meets a young Gretzky after a little league hockey game, telling him, 'You could go far, my boy! You've got what it takes!'"

Derek's feelings are not unusual for young writers. Finding a mentor can be a wonderful solution to this dilemma.

A mentor is an adult who can help young people develop in a particular career area. Mentors for young writers can be teachers, professors, parents, and other writers. Here are some suggestions on how to work with a mentor.

- You must feel safe with a mentor. The point of a mentorship is to develop *your* writing, not to have someone else's thoughts on writing forced on you. Do you feel that you are being coached to develop and improve your own style? If not, a particular mentor might not be right for you.

- You must feel that you are getting honest feedback. For example, is your mentor giving you a true estimate of how long it will take for a piece of writing to be developed into publishable material, or even to get published? Most of the short stories I see may be ready after a month's hard work, and a novel may take anywhere from six months to a year, depending on the manuscript and how much time the young writer can put into it.

- If you have decided to work in a specific genre, it is usually best to find a mentor who has been published in that genre.

If you are interested in learning how to find and work with a mentor, you may want to read this book:

- *Mentorship: The Essential Guide for Schools and Business* by Jill Reilly (Dayton, OH: Ohio Psychology Press, 1992). Written for adults, this book contains good information for students.

Celebrate Special Days

In your own country, state, or province, there may be special days and weeks that celebrate writing. See what special days you can find in your community. Your librarian should be able to help you.

In the United States, there is a National Children's Book Week in November. In Canada, there is a National Book Week in April. Also, P.E.N. International celebrates International Writers' Day each year in March on a specially chosen day.

Make the Most of Author Visits

Authors are often invited to schools and libraries to give readings from their works *or* to give writing workshops. (They usually don't do both during the same visit.) If you ever have a chance to meet an author personally, you will want to be prepared. Put together a list of questions you would like to have answered, and think seriously about what sort of feedback you would like on your writing – provided that the author will be able to give you feedback.

What can you do to make the most of an author visit? Here are five suggestions.

1. **Find out from your teacher (or the person planning the visit) if the author will be there for a *reading* or a *workshop*.** If the answer is a workshop, ask if the author will have time to give you feedback on a particular piece of writing you are working on or have finished. Will you need to submit a copy in advance, so the author can read it before the workshop? (If the answer is a reading, you probably will not be able to get feedback on your writing.)

2. **If you have a piece of writing you would like the author to read, read through it yourself ahead of time and estimate how long it will take the author to read.** While you might like the author to read your whole novel, it is not fair to expect him or her to do so.

    If it will take the author one or two minutes to read your writing, you can ask if it is possible to get some feedback during the workshop. For example, one or two poems or an excerpt from a story or novel would work well. (When you request that an author read your work and give you feedback, be prepared to accept a "no" in response, and do it gracefully.) If it will take the author anywhere from 10 minutes to half an hour to read your piece of writing, guess what? Impossible! So what do you do? Highlight one section of one or two pages you actually want feedback on. Or come up with your own idea, but be aware of time limitations.

3. **If you are asking the author for feedback on pages of a story you have written, be prepared to give a very brief, precise summary of your story.** The author may ask you, "What is your story about?" The author is not asking you to recite your story from beginning to end, or to recite a complicated plot outline that will take 15 minutes.

Try to condense your story into three or four sentences. Make sure that your summary takes less than a minute to say. Practice saying it to yourself in the mirror, or write it down so you can read it easily and quickly.

For example, at the front of Roald Dahl's book, *Matilda,* the publisher put this brief summary: "Matilda applies her untapped mental powers to rid the school of the evil, child-hating headmistress, Miss Turnbull, to restore her nice teacher, Miss Honey, to financial security." If you are familiar with *Matilda*, you know that this is a very brief outline. But it conveys the storyline precisely and succinctly.

4. **Be clear about what you want to learn from the author.** Try not to show a piece of writing simply to get assurance that you have talent. If you want to share a piece, fine. If you want help with a technical problem – if somehow your description doesn't seem to work in a particular place, or the dialogue falls flat – that is fine, too.

5. **If you feel shy about talking to the author, remember why the author is there.** Authors, poets, and illustrators go out in public because they care very much about stories and books and are thrilled to meet other writers. Otherwise, they simply wouldn't be there.

More Options for Feedback from Authors

The young writers I know who have had exposure to professional coaching by authors have raved about the experience. There's a depth, mastery, and passion that certain authors who love to work with young writers bring to their sessions.

In fact, there is a rare type of excitement in store for both parties. On the one hand, young writers can have their work and thoughts taken seriously, which helps them to move on to the next level of their craft. On the other, professional authors can share the techniques, tricks, and experiences of their craft with someone who is deeply interested. As Charles Montpetit, a celebrated French-Canadian writer of science fiction for young adults, wrote about the week he spent at the International Young Authors' Camp: "I could have withstood another year of their company and not have plumbed the depth of their competence.... I've been jarred out of my complacency by the dedication and potential of young writers."

Aspiring writers need exposure to authors. In some states, provinces, and counties, there are programs where you can actually take a manuscript to an author and get feedback on it. Usually these programs are offered through libraries or universities and are called "Writer-in-Residence" programs. (Sometimes they are called "Writer-in-the-Libraries" or "Writer-in-the-Schools.") In an effort to encourage teachers and students to use their facilities for creative writing, education officers at various art galleries, museums, and even zoos have begun to offer on-site writing programs. My program in the Jersey Zoo, Channel Islands, is called "Writer-in-the-Zoo." My program at the Tower of London in England is called "Writer-in-the-Tower."

Another option is to look for an author who works well with young writers and ask him or her to coach you on a private basis for a fee. While this system is well in place with music education (in particular, piano teachers), the idea of a private writing coach is still new to most young writers, their parents, and teachers. One young author took her coaching so seriously that she decided to spend all of her birthday money for coaching on short stories. I recommended a short story writer to her who gave her feedback on a number of her stories. This determined young writer went on to win a major contest in picture book writing and had her first book published at the age of 19! Her name is Kristin Pedersen; the title of her book is *The Shadow Shop*. It was published by Landmark Editions in 1994. You can read what Kristin says about her experience on pages 97–98.

Imagine that you discover the work of a particular author. You read it, you like it very much – and you discover that the author lives in your community. You tell your parents what you have learned and ask if it might be possible for you to work with the author. Explain that you would like the author to read your writing and give you constructive criticism. Be aware that authors are professionals and will most likely charge a rate equivalent to that of a good music teacher.

If you can't find a private writing coach, you might try to attend a young writers' workshop or camp, where it is possible to get feedback on longer pieces of work. Working with a professional writer, whether at a summer camp or workshop or on an individual basis, can be a wonderful experience for a young writer.

If you can't work with a professional author in person, you can still learn about writing from published authors. Many fine authors have written books about writing. Here are a few titles you may want to look for. Ask your librarian to recommend others.

- *The Art of Fiction: Notes on Craft for Young Writers* by John Gardner (New York: Random House, 1991).

- *On Writing Well,* 4th edition, by William Zinsser (New York: HarperCollins, 1990).

- *The Passionate, Accurate Story: Making Your Heart's Truth into Literature* by Carol Bly (Minneapolis: Milkweed Editions, 1990).

- *Starting from Scratch: A Different Kind of Writers' Manual* by Rita Mae Brown (New York: Bantam Books, 1989).

- *Writing Down the Bones: Freeing the Writer Within* by Natalie Goldberg (Boston: Shambhala, 1986).

If you enjoy reading quotations by writers about writing, you might look for these books:

- *Good Advice on Writing: Great Quotations from Writers Past and Present on How to Write Well* by William Safire and Leonard Safire (New York: Simon & Schuster, 1992).

- *Shoptalk: Learning to Write with Writers* by Donald M. Murray (Portsmouth, NH: Boynton/Cook Publishers, 1990).

- *Writers on Writing* by Jon Winokur (Philadelphia: Running Press, 1990).

- *The Writers' Quotation Book: A Literary Companion,* edited by James Charlton (New York: Penguin Books, 1986).

Support from Librarians and Teachers

Librarians and teachers can both be important sources of support for young writers. Your librarian might have all kinds of information regarding interesting books and organizations. Your English teacher might give you the flexibility to turn a creative writing assignment into a writing-for-publication assignment.

A lot of the writing you do at this time is most likely for classroom assignments. Why not see if you can use some of it for other purposes? Following are a few questions and answers on this topic.

Question: My teacher has asked for a 1,000-word story. I want to do a 2,000-word story because that is the required word count for a contest I want to enter.

Answer: There are two possibilities here. You can perceive the word count as an exercise in self-discipline and write a tighter story. Or you can explain to your teacher why you want to do a longer story and see if you can get special permission. If you can't, you'll just have to do the longer story on your own time.

Question: When my teacher edits my work, it ends up being totally changed, and I don't like it anymore.

Answer: Talk to your teacher and explain why it is important that you keep your story a particular way. (This is good practice, because an editor at a publishing house may do the exact same thing to you. You need to build your skills of explaining why certain parts of your writing work. At the same time, be prepared to concede when a teacher – or an editor – has a good point.)

Question: My teacher doesn't believe that a piece of writing is my own.

Answer: Always keep all of your drafts and notes as you work. If a teacher ever questions whether a piece of writing is really yours (and let's hope this never happens), show your parents your drafts and notes and explain the problem. Arrange to meet with the teacher and ask your parents to accompany you to school.

Question: My teacher has difficulty with my writing assignments because they contain lots of dark imagery, violence, and unusual dialogue. She has even complained to my mother about it.

Answer: You need to know that you are not alone. Individual schools and teachers have their own limits on what is considered acceptable in creative writing. You can try taking in samples of work by professional writers that seem similar to your work, as well as books about genres, and see if your teacher would be willing to discuss the level of violence, language, etc. that is acceptable on school assignments. Or you may have to explore your fullest creative work outside the classroom. Find publishing markets for the type of writing you do, and tone down your style for classroom assignments. Many professional writers have to adapt their writing style for different markets, so this might be good practice for you!

Making Connections

It is probably easier and more useful for young writers to join a local writing organization than a national professional writing organization. Check with other writers in your area to find out about organizations that might be open to you. Ask at your library or bookstore. You might find an organization nearby that welcomes young writers.

If you like, you might see if it is possible to join a national professional writing organization. Even if it is not possible for you to join right now, you may be able to attend meetings as a "guest" if you find a member who is willing to take you. Following are partial listings of such organizations by country (Australia, Canada, England, and the United States). Membership usually requires some publishing track record, but some organizations have membership categories open to unpublished writers.

Professional writing organizations produce excellent materials on contracts, current markets, local writing seminars, grants, awards, etc. These materials are usually available for a small fee. Please do not ask staff members for editorial advice or answers to questions you can easily find yourself, with a bit of research.

Read through the list pertaining to your country and find one organization that you would like to know more about. Write to the organization and request general information about membership, publications, and workshops for young writers in your area. When you receive the information, place the requirements for membership in your Writer's Notebook.

Then read through the list of publications and decide if there are any of interest to you. You can also take the list to your teacher or librarian and ask if they would like to order copies. You can also see if there are any local workshops in your area. It is important to remember that most of these organizations will help you – even if you are not a member – to understand your first publishing contract.

Australia

The Australian Society of Authors Ltd., P.O. Box 450, Milsons Point, NSW 2061, Australia.

Poetry Society of Australia, Suite 4, 245 Chalmers St., Redfern, Sydney, NSW 2000, Australia.

Canada

Canadian Society of Children's Authors, Illustrators, and Performers, 542 Mt. Pleasant Road, Suite 103, Toronto, Ontario, M4S 2M7, Canada. Most of CANSCAIP's members are adults, but they do accept teenage "friends." All friends receive the organization's newsletter.

The League of Canadian Poets, 24 Ryerson Avenue, Toronto, Ontario, M5T 2P3, Canada.

The Periodical Writers' Association of Canada, 24 Ryerson Avenue, Toronto, Ontario, M5T 2P3, Canada.

The Playwrights Union of Canada, 54 Wolseley Street, Toronto, Ontario, M5T 1A5, Canada.

Writers Guild of Canada, 35 McCaul Street, Suite 300, Toronto, Ontario, M5T 1V7, Canada.

The Writers' Union of Canada, 24 Ryerson Avenue, Toronto, Ontario, M5T 2P3, Canada. Contact them for a list of provincial writing organizations.

England

The Poetry Society, 21 Earls Court Square, London SW5 9DE, England.

The Society of Authors, 84 Drayton Gardens, London SW10 9SB, England.

The Writers' Guild of Great Britain, 430 Edgware Road, London W2 1EH, England.

For a complete listing of professional associations in Great Britain, refer to *The Writer's Handbook* (Macmillan/PEN, updated annually).

United States

The Authors' Guild, Inc., 300 West 42nd Street, 29th Floor, New York, NY 10036, U.S.A.

National Writers Association, 1450 S. Havana, Suite 424, Aurora, CO 80012, U.S.A. The National Writers Club is open to young writers. It offers students access to all of their services at a low membership fee.

The Society of Children's Book Writers and Illustrators, 22736 Vanowen Street, Suite 106, West Hills, CA 91307, U.S.A.

Other Countries

For information about professional writing organizations in other countries, see "Literary Associations" in *International Literary Marketplace* (New York: R.R. Bowker, published annually).

RECOMMENDED READING

- *Under the Eye of the Clock* by Christopher Nolan (Oxford: Isis, 1988). In his autobiography, Christopher Nolan tells how he overcame some of the hardships of being severely handicapped and went on to become a highly respected poet. He shows how working with one's parents and friends can really help a young writer's career.

Many writers have written about their lives, experiences, and careers. Here are just a few recommendations. Ask your librarian for others.

- *One Writer's Beginnings* by Eudora Welty (Cambridge, MA: Harvard University Press, 1990). The Pulitzer Prize-winning author tells how her family and her surroundings shaped her personality and her writing.

- *The Writing Life* by Annie Dillard (New York: HarperPerennial, 1990). A slim and powerful book about writing by the Pulitzer Prize-winning author of *Pilgrim at Tinker Creek.*

If you are interested in reading interviews with writers, you might try one or more of these titles:

- *Conversations with American Writers* by Charles Ruas (New York: Alfred A. Knopf, 1985). Conversational interviews with Toni Morrison, Eudora Welty, Truman Capote, Joseph Heller, Susan Sontag, Tennessee Williams, and others.

- *Winged Words: American Indian Writers Speak* by Laura Coltelli (Lincoln, NE: University of Nebraska Press, 1990).

- *Writers at Work: The* Paris Review *Interviews.* Beginning in 1953, the *Paris Review,* a literary magazine, published a series of interviews with contemporary writers. Currently there are nine volumes in this series, published by Viking Penguin and Penguin Books. Some of the writers interviewed include E.M. Forster, William Faulkner, Aldous Huxley, Ernest Hemingway, Katherine Anne Porter, Ralph Ellison, James Jones, Lillian Hellman, John Steinbeck, Eudora Welty, Joyce Carol Oates, Isaac Bashevis Singer, Joseph Heller, Kurt Vonnegut, Jr., Nadine Gordimer, Gabriel Garcia

Marquez, Milan Kundera, May Sarton, Raymond Carver,
E.B. White, Elie Wiesel, Anita Brookner, and John Irving.

There are many other sources of interesting reading for young writers,
including biographies of famous actors, introductions to adaptations
of books for the stage, and compilations of song lyrics. If you need
some humorous encouragement along the way, here are a few books
I have enjoyed by (and about) a violinist, an actor/director, and a stage
and movie actress who landed on the road to fame in their 20s:

- *Always Playing* by Nigel Kennedy (London: George Weidenfeld &
  Nicolson Ltd., 1991).

- *Beginnings* by Kenneth Branagh (London: Chatto & Windus, 1989).

- *Maggie Smith: A Particular Star* by Michael Coveney (London:
  Victor Gollanz Ltd., 1992).

READING CHALLENGE

- *The Closing of the American Mind* by Allan Bloom (New York:
  Simon & Schuster, 1988).

I know that the moment I say, "You should be at least 16 years old to
take this reading challenge," some of you will go ahead and try to read
this anyway. Be sure to read Chapter 3, which contains an excellent discussion about books in society as well as a gold mine of recommended
classics. But please be aware that this is a *very* adult book – so adult
that I've had reviewers absolutely puzzled as to how a young writer
could even attempt to read it. Well, not only have I seen a 16-year-old
dive head first into parts of it and come up singing its praises, but I've
read aloud parts of Chapter 3 to writing campers ages 11–19, and they
haven't had a problem comprehending what the author is saying.
I leave it in your hands.

- *Developing Talent in Young People* by Benjamin S. Bloom
  (New York: Ballantine, 1985).

If you are interested in finding out about how talent development
occurs with young people your own age, try reading certain chapters

in this thick but very readable book, originally written for adults. What's nice about it is that you can flip through it and choose a particular section based on an age group or talent area. I found the most striking comparisons to developing young writers in the section on Sculptors.

I have found that many parents of promising young writers are interested in how they can offer support, especially if they are not writers themselves. Your parents may also want to read this book.

"As a writer you are free.
You are about the freest person that ever was.
Your freedom is what you have bought
with your solitude, your loneliness. You are in the
country where you make up the rules, the laws.
You are both dictator and obedient populace.
It is a country nobody has ever explored before.
It is up to you to make the maps, to build the cities.
Nobody else in the world can do it, or ever could
do it, or ever will be able to do it again."

Ursula K. Le Guin in LANGUAGE OF THE NIGHT

A Few Final Words...

By now, you will have had a chance to see that the path you tread in becoming a writer is not any different in certain respects than the pursuit of any other occupation or sport. It takes time, self-knowledge, knowledge of different types of writing, and a lot of practice. Most of all, it takes a lot of YOU.

Through working with the Writer's Notebook exercises, you will have had the opportunity to become aware of what is really important to you and what you want out of your writing. No goal is too big or too small. It is my hope that at any time in your writing life, you will remember the "small steps":

- answering the question, "Why do you write?"
- choosing one or two genres to specialize in
- understanding the rules of different genres
- refining characters, dialogue, and settings
- getting support and mentoring, and
- choosing wisely the best places for you to be published.

Rather than just reading and writing the occasional piece of fiction, you now should have clear, practical ideas of what you need to do if you want to improve your writing skills.

Remember, there is room for your voice. Be patient. Believe in your dreams and your ability – and ask for help when you need it.

In becoming a writer, there is much work involved, but it is a type of work that if you love it, it doesn't feel like work at all. It feels like life.

"Putting a book together is interesting
and exhilarating. It is sufficiently difficult
and complex that it engages all your intelligence.
It is life at its most free...if you are
fortunate enough to be able to try it."
Annie Dillard, author of PILGRIM AT TINKER CREEK,
winner of the Pulitzer Prize

Writer's Notebook: Doing the Exercises

Copy this page and slip it into your Writer's Notebook as a reminder to do the exercises. Check off each exercise as you complete it.

CHAPTER ONE: THE LAND OF THE IMAGINATION

___ Rate Yourself
___ An Afternoon with Your Favorite Authors

CHAPTER TWO: IDENTIFYING THE WRITER WITHIN

___ Writer's Bluff
___ The Reason You Write
___ A Peace Break
___ What Do They Really Mean When They Say...
___ Rate Your Skills

CHAPTER THREE: LEARNING ABOUT GENRES

___ Where Does Your Writing Come From?
___ Writing What You Write Best
___ A Day in the Life

CHAPTER FOUR: PLAYING WITH YOUR IMAGINATION

___ Making a Timetable
___ The Character Sheet

___ Improving Characters and Dialogue
___ Gender Communication
___ Mind Stretchers
___ Improving Settings
___ Rate Your Writing

CHAPTER FIVE: FINDING THE RIGHT PUBLISHERS

___ Checking Out Libraries and Bookstores
___ Finding the Right Publishers

CHAPTER SIX: PREPARING YOUR MANUSCRIPT

___ Manuscript Submission Checklist
___ Preparing Your Bio Sheet

CHAPTER SEVEN: YOUR MONEY AND YOUR PUBLISHING RIGHTS

___ Write Your Own Budget

CHAPTER EIGHT: CONNECTING WITH THE WRITING COMMUNITY

___ A Library of Classics
___ Making Connections

Index

About the Author

A CAREER COUNSELING QUIZ Janet E. Grant took in high school advised her to become a forest ranger. Since then, she has led writing workshops outside, and, where possible, in the most unusual places – to date, the Jersey Zoo, Channel Islands; The Tower of London; and on the borders of Algonquin Park, Canada. She is happiest writing outdoors, by water, or in cafés with pen in one hand and coffee cup in the other. Her only known allergies are shopping and purses.

Her writing friends describe her as "wacky" and "a producer," one member of the press describes her as "a path-breaking writing teacher," and her un-artsy friends think she has a very unusual imagination.

Born in Toronto, Canada, Janet grew up in a large family where her parents encouraged each child to have fun and develop their own talent in everything from squash (the game, not the vegetable) to urban planning. This was the foundation for her work in respecting teenagers' different interests and talents. She spent one summer as a student journalist for *Ontario Tennis* magazine and chaperone to the provincial junior team. She graduated from Sussex University with an Hon. B.A. in English Literature and started leading corporate writing workshops in Canada at the tender age of 23.

As a private consultant, Janet has spent hundreds of hours one-on-one with teenagers, helping them with creative writing and school assignments, and has lectured at universities and schools across Canada. She founded the Canadian Young Authors' Camp (subsequently renamed the International Young Authors' Camp) in 1989 and served as its director until 1992. In 1993, she left Canada to pursue an interest in children's musicals in London, England. In 1994, she started to shadow David Wood, considered "the national children's playwright," and she is currently working on a book with him, *David Wood's Guide to Writing, Directing, and Acting – Theatre for Children.* She is also the author of *The Writing Coach: Strategies for Helping Students Develop Their Own Writing Voice; The Kid's Green Plan: How to Make Your Own Plan to Save the Environment;* and four biographies.

Janet's best sport is tennis, but she also hits a mean 3-wood ("the closest golf club to a tennis racquet"). She lives in London, England, but spends several months each year in Canada and the United States.

If you are interested in having Janet Grant present workshops on writing to your group, and/or having her act as a consultant in the development of a writing program in your area, please write to her c/o Free Spirit Publishing Inc., 400 First Avenue North, Suite 616, Minneapolis, MN 55401-1730, U.S.A.

MORE FREE SPIRIT BOOKS

THE BEST OF FREE SPIRIT®: FIVE YEARS OF AWARD-WINNING NEWS & VIEWS ON GROWING UP
by the Free Spirit Editors
Hundreds of articles, tips, and cartoons on topics including "Self-Awareness and Self-Esteem," "Making a Difference," "Diversity," "Family and Friends," "Study Skills and Test-Taking Tips," and more. Everything is reproducible for home and classroom use. Ages 10 and up.
$23.95; 276 pp.; illust.; s/c; 8 1/2" x 11"

CREATING PORTFOLIOS FOR SUCCESS IN SCHOOL, WORK, AND LIFE
by Martin Kimeldorf
This creative, hands-on workbook guides students step by step through the process of producing meaningful, useful portfolios that show their interests, abilities, and accomplishments. The **Teacher's Guide** introduces the activities, suggests ways to adapt portfolios for various grade levels and students with special needs, offers advice on evaluating portfolios, and more. Ages 12 and up.
Student Workbook: $11.95; 104 pp.; illust.; s/c; 8 1/2" x 11"
Teacher's Guide: $12.95; 64 pp.; illust.; s/c; 8 1/2" x 11"
10 Student Workbooks: $99.00 (over 15% savings!)

EXCITING WRITING, SUCCESSFUL SPEAKING: ACTIVITIES TO MAKE LANGUAGE COME ALIVE IN THE CLASSROOM
by Martin Kimeldorf
This dynamic alternative to traditional composition books makes writing fun and meaningful for students at all ability levels. Dozens of creative, hands-on activities teach essential communication skills while keeping students interested and involved. The **Teacher's Guide** contains over 20 reproducible handouts to use in the lessons. Ages 11 and up.
Student Workbook: $14.95; 216 pp.; illust.; s/c; 8 1/2" x 11"
Teacher's Guide: $19.95; 112 pp.; s/c; 8 1/2" x 11"
10 Student Workbooks: $127.00 (over 15% savings!)

To place an order, or to request a free catalog of SELF-HELP FOR KIDS® materials, write or call:

Free Spirit Publishing Inc.
400 First Avenue North, Suite 616
Minneapolis, MN 55401-1730
Toll-free (800) 735-7323, Local (612) 338-2068
Fax (612) 337-5050